BIG-NOTE PIANO

2ND EDITION

THE BEATLES

COLLECTION

ISBN 978-0-7935-9494-8

HAL•LEONARD
CORPORATION
7777 W. BLUEMOUND RD. P.O. BOX 13819 MILWAUKEE, WI 5

D0813585

Visit Hal Leonard Online at
www.halleonard.com

ACROSS THE UNIVERSE

Words and Music by JOHN LENNON
and PAUL McCARTNEY

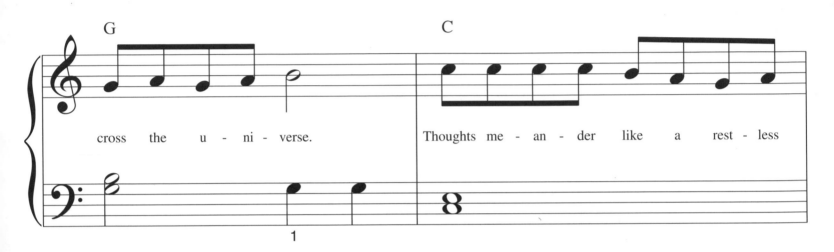

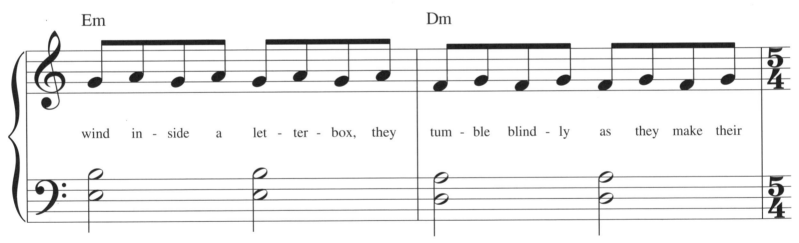

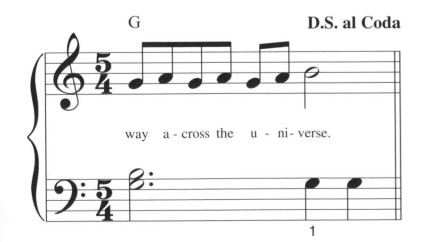

ALL MY LOVING

Words and Music by JOHN LENNON
and PAUL McCARTNEY

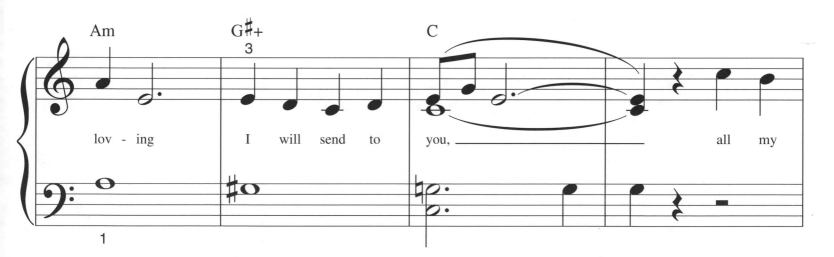

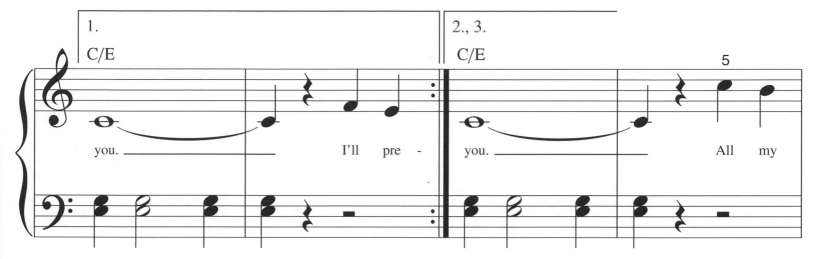

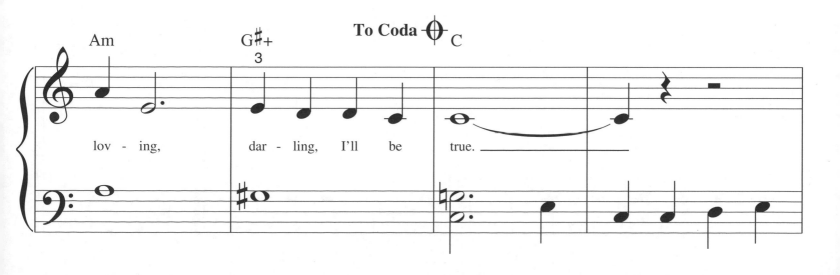

ALL YOU NEED IS LOVE

Words and Music by JOHN LENNON
and PAUL McCARTNEY

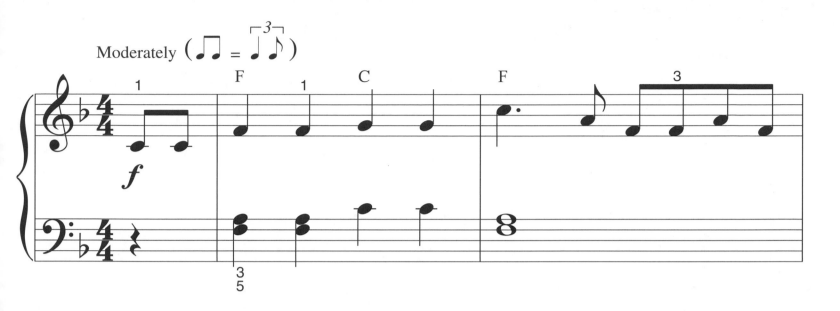

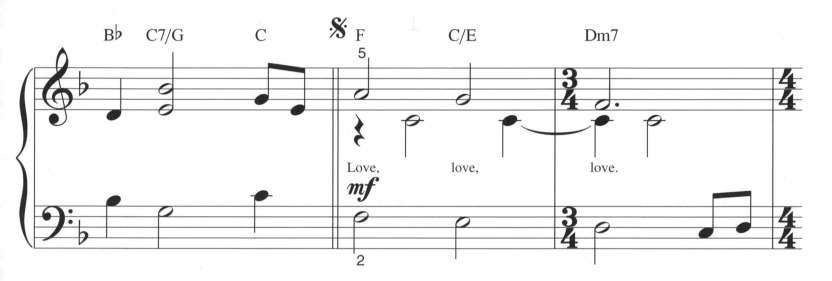

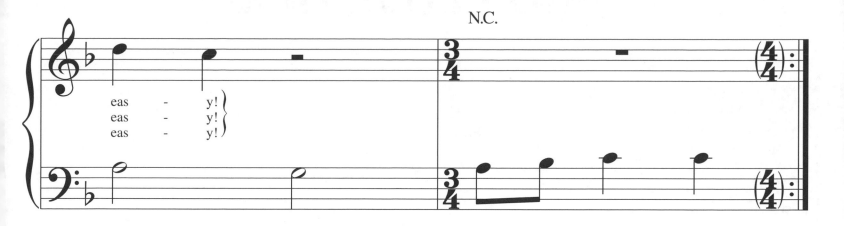

N.C.

eas - y!
eas - y!
eas - y!

All you need is love,

all you need is

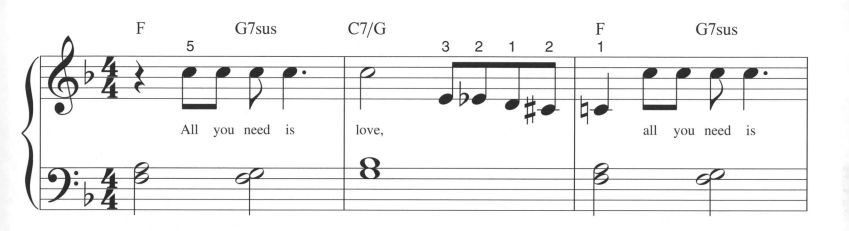

love,

all you need is love, love.

To Coda ⊕   D.S. al Coda
(no repeat)

CODA

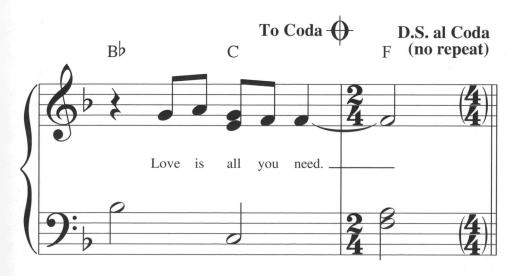

Love is all you need.

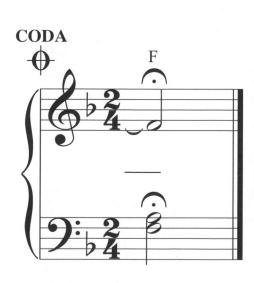

AND I LOVE HER

Words and Music by JOHN LENNON
and PAUL McCARTNEY

ASK ME WHY

Words and Music by JOHN LENNON
and PAUL McCARTNEY

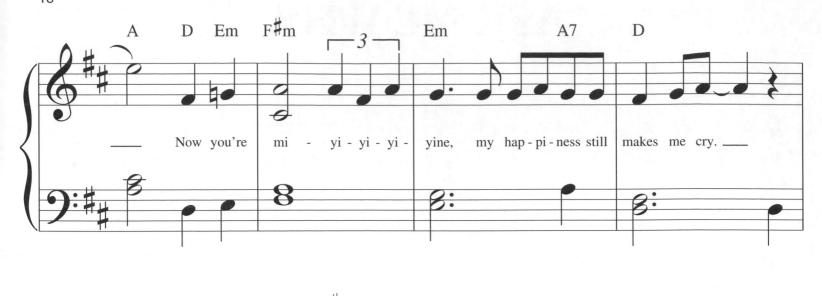

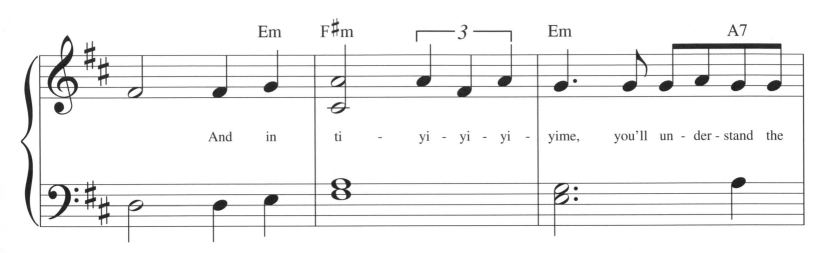

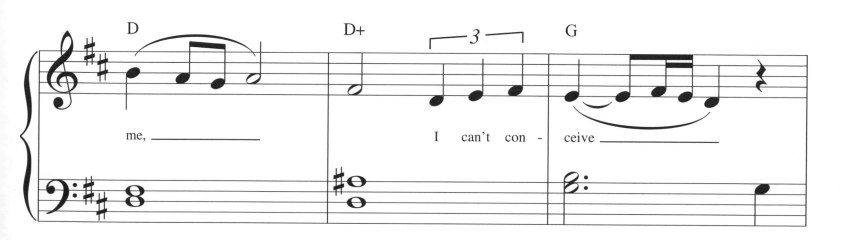

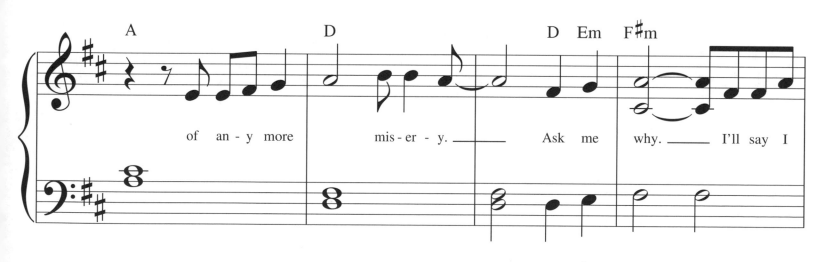

BECAUSE

Words and Music by JOHN LENNON
and PAUL McCARTNEY

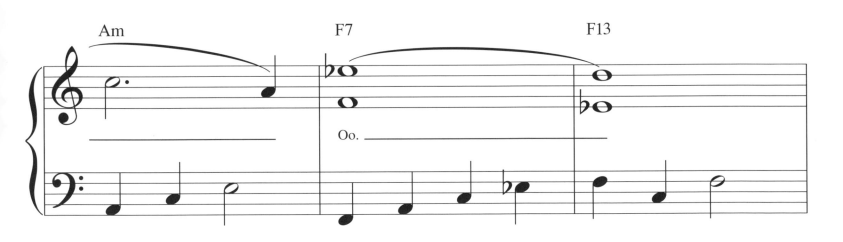

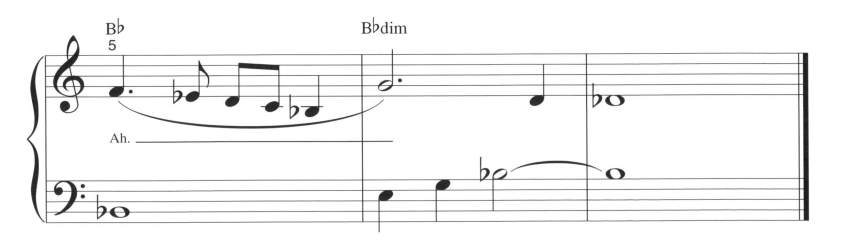

CARRY THAT WEIGHT

Words and Music by JOHN LENNON
and PAUL McCARTNEY

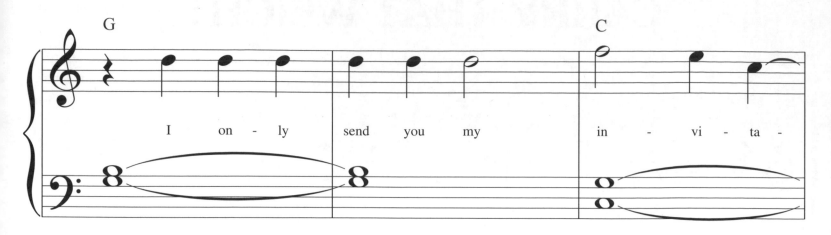

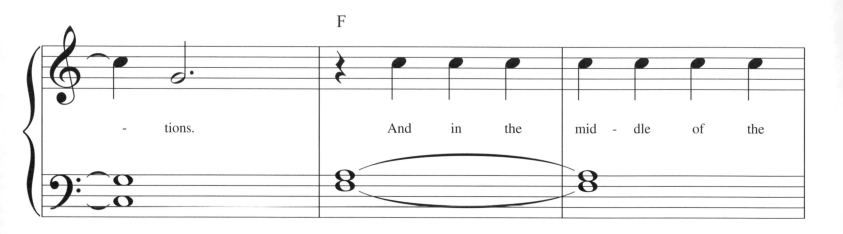

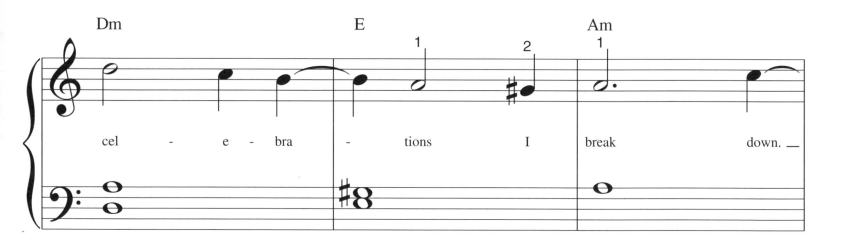

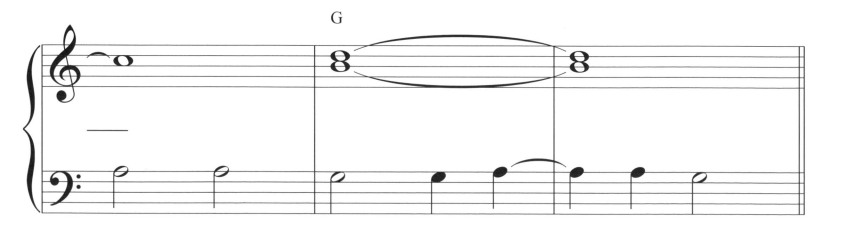

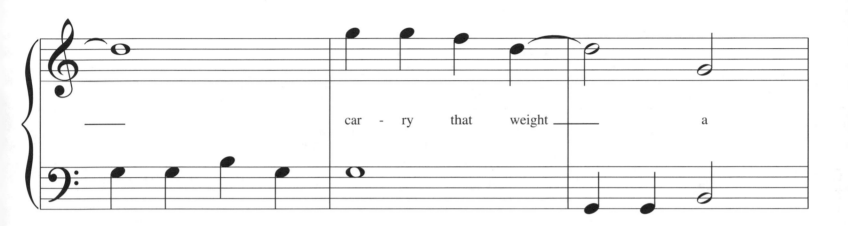

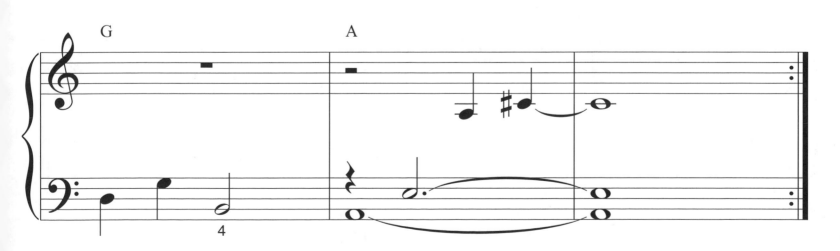

BLACKBIRD

Words and Music by JOHN LENNON
and PAUL McCARTNEY

Black-bird, sing-ing in the dead of
Black-bird, sing-ing in the dead of

night,
night,
take these bro-ken wings and learn to
take these sunk-en eyes and learn to

fly;
see;

all your life ____
all your life ____
you were on-ly
you were on-ly
wait-ing for this mo-ment to a-
wait-ing for this mo-ment to be

rise.

CAN'T BUY ME LOVE

Words and Music by JOHN LENNON
and PAUL McCARTNEY

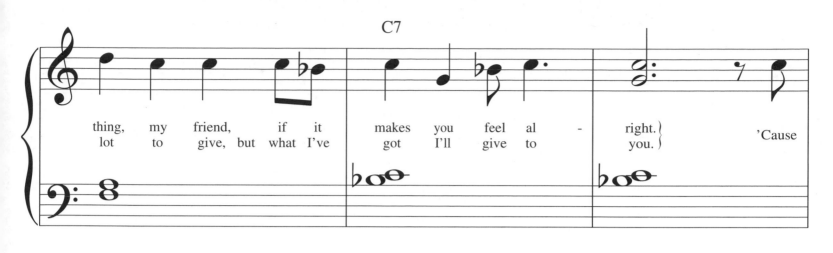

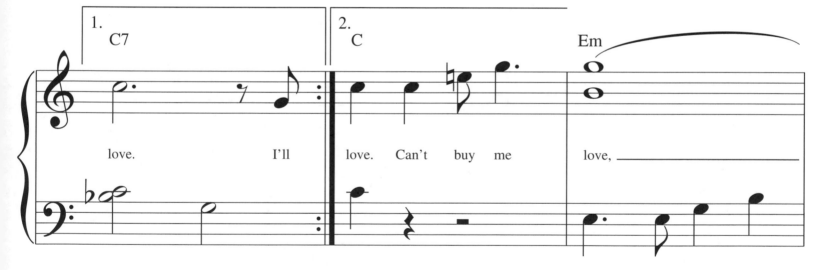

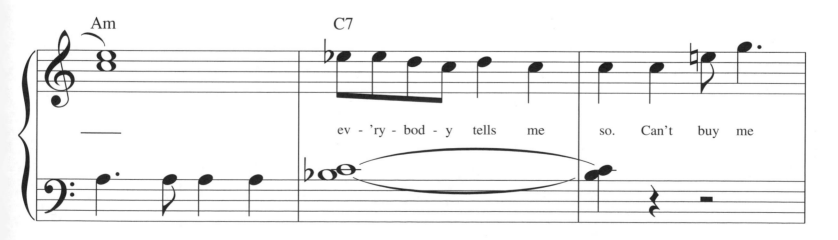

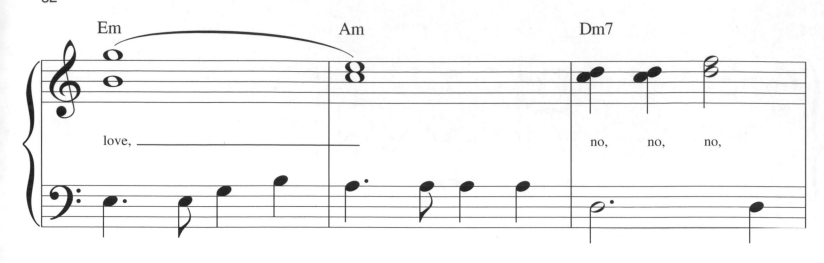

love, _____   no,   no,   no,

no!   Say you don't need no   dia - mond rings   and

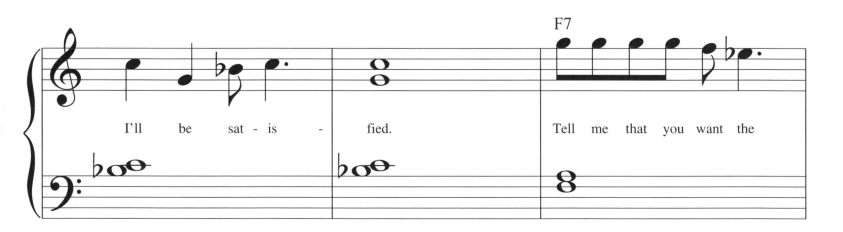

I'll   be   sat - is -   fied.   Tell   me   that   you   want   the

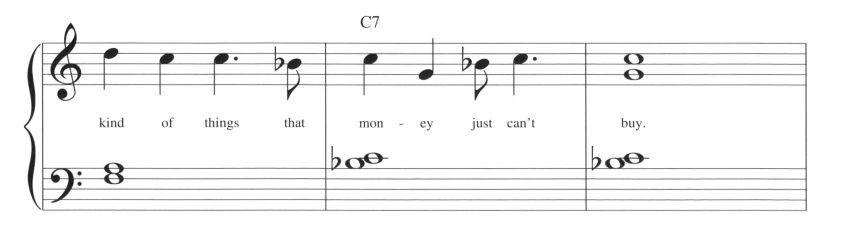

kind   of   things   that   mon - ey   just   can't   buy.

COME TOGETHER

Words and Music by JOHN LENNON
and PAUL McCARTNEY

Got to be a jok - er, he just do what he please. ___

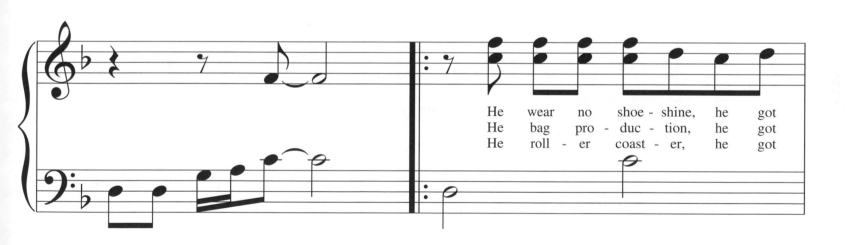

He wear no shoe - shine, he got
He bag pro - duc - tion, he got
He roll - er coast - er, he got

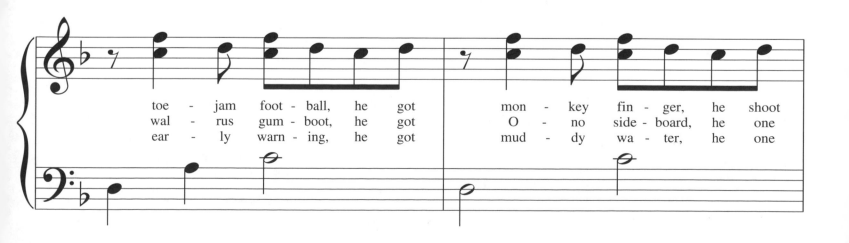

toe - jam foot - ball, he got   mon - key fin - ger, he shoot
wal - rus gum - boot, he got   O - no side - board, he one
ear - ly warn - ing, he got   mud - dy wa - ter, he one

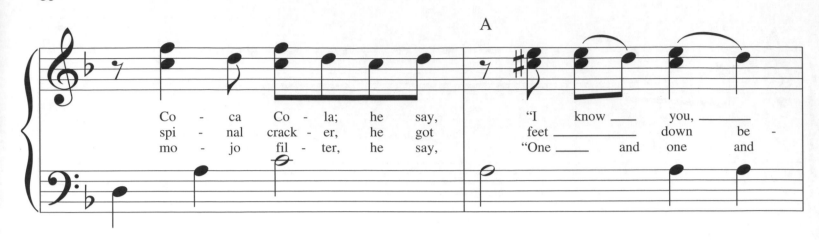

Co - ca Co - la; he say,
spi - nal crack - er, he got
mo - jo fil - ter, he say,

"I know _____ you, _____
feet _____ down be -
"One _____ and one and

you know me." _____
low his knee. _____
one is three." _____

One thing I can tell you is you
Hold you in his arm - chair, you can
Got to be good look - ing 'cause he

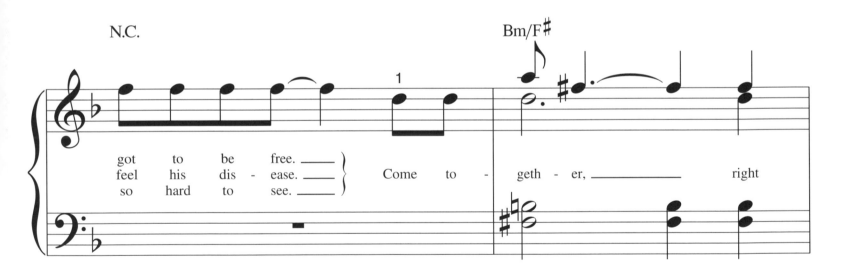

got to be free. _____
feel his dis - ease. _____
so hard to see. _____

Come to - geth - er, _____ right

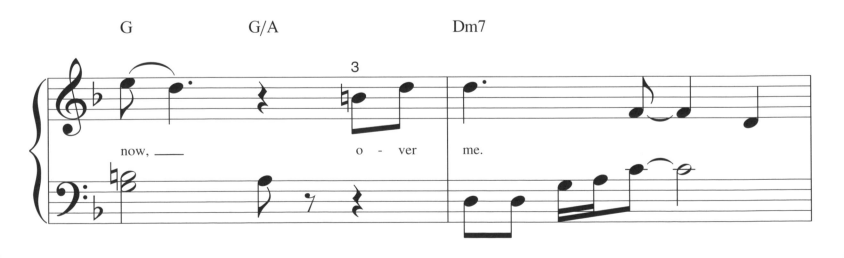

now, _____ o - ver me.

DAY TRIPPER

Words and Music by JOHN LENNON
and PAUL McCARTNEY

Moderate Rock

Got a good rea - son
She's a big teas - er,
Tried __ to please __ her,

for tak - ing the eas - y way out;
she took me half __ the way there;
she on - ly played __ one night stands;

got a good rea - son
she's a big teas - er,
tried __ to please __ her,

for tak - ing the eas - y way
she took me half __ the way
she on - ly played __ one night

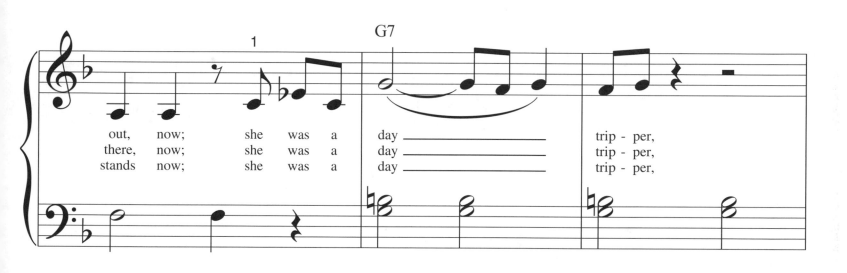

out, now; she was a day _____ trip - per,
there, now; she was a day _____ trip - per,
stands now; she was a day _____ trip - per,

one - way tick - et, yeah! ____ It took me so _____
one - way tick - et, yeah! ____ It took me so _____
Sun - day driv - er, yeah! ____ It took me so _____

long _____ to find out, and I found out!
long _____ to find out, and I found out!
long _____ to find out, and I found out!

out!

Ah. _____

D.C. al Coda

CODA

C

out!

F7

F

DO YOU WANT TO KNOW A SECRET?

Words and Music by JOHN LENNON
and PAUL McCARTNEY

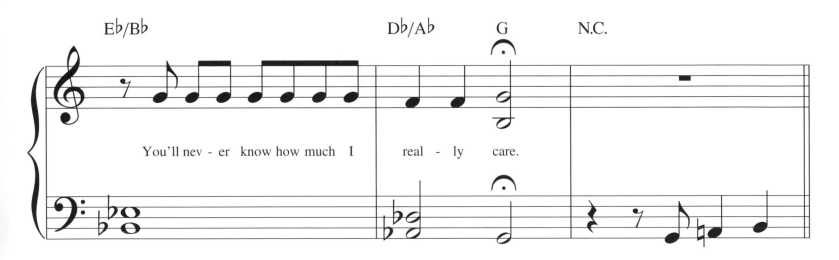

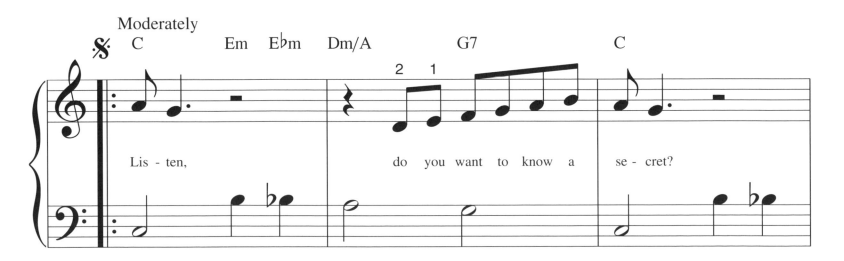

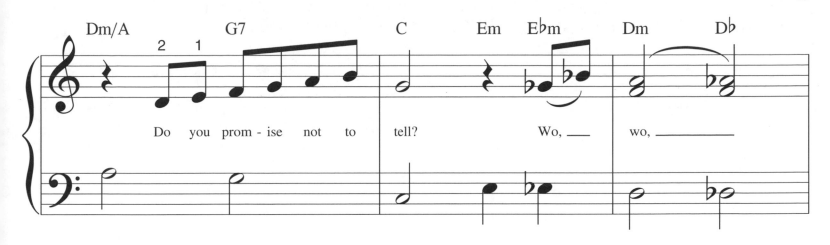

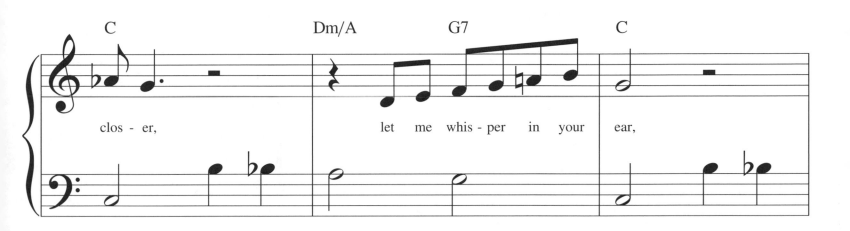

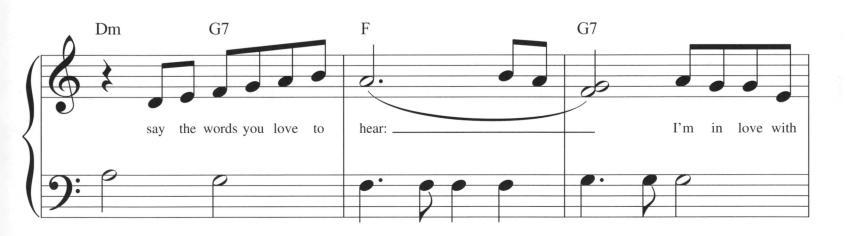

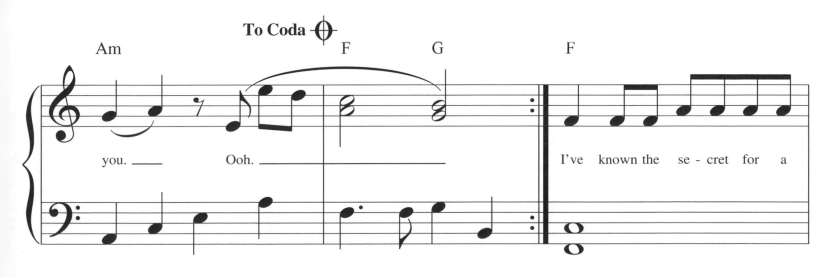

44

DON'T LET ME DOWN

Words and Music by JOHN LENNON
and PAUL McCARTNEY

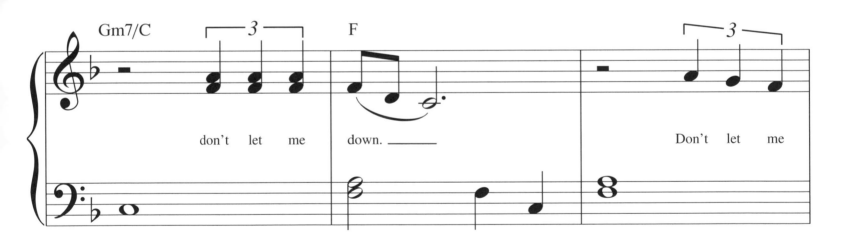

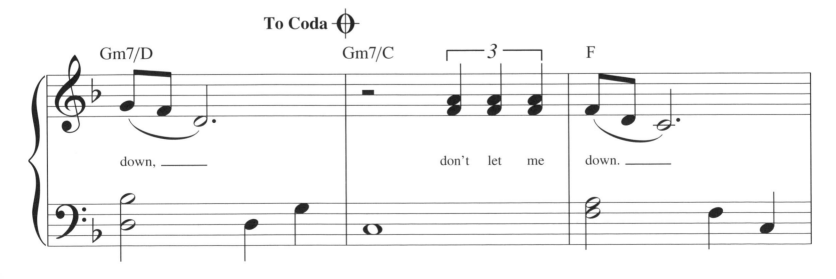

I'm in love for the first time. Don't you know it's gon - na

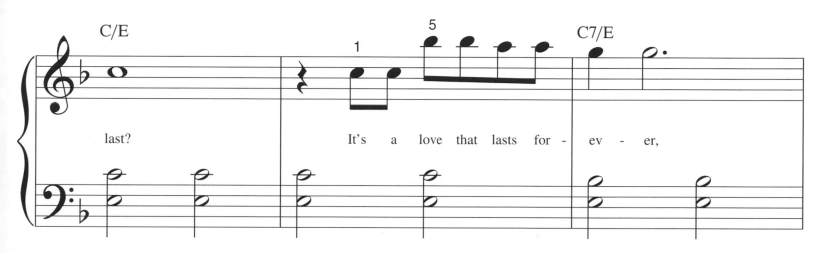

last? It's a love that lasts for - ev - er,

it's a love that had no past. Don't let me

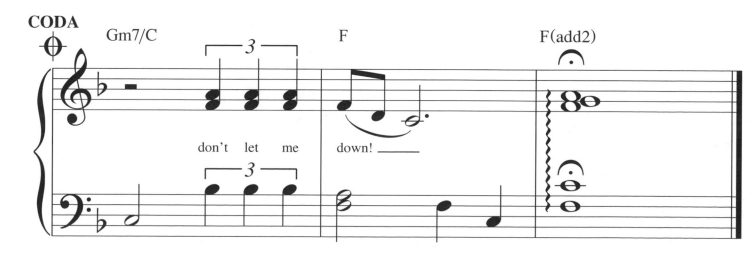

don't let me down!

DRIVE MY CAR

Words and Music by JOHN LENNON
and PAUL McCARTNEY

With a beat

I asked a girl what she want-ed to be, ___
I told the girl that my pros-pects were good, ___
I told the girl I could start right a-way, ___

and she said, "Ba-by, can't you see? ___
and she said, "Ba-by, it's un-der-stood. ___
and she said, "Listen, babe, I got some-thing to say. ___

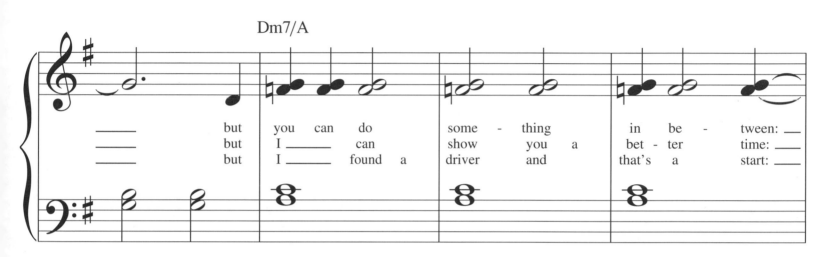

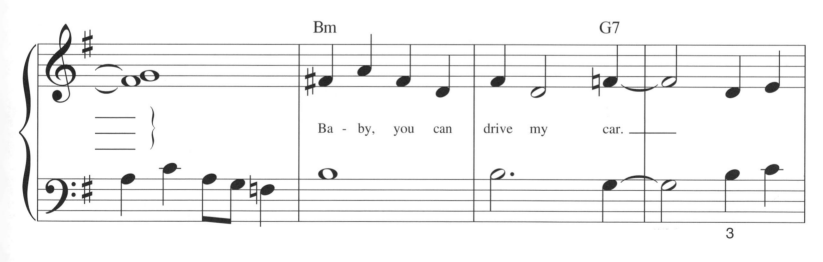

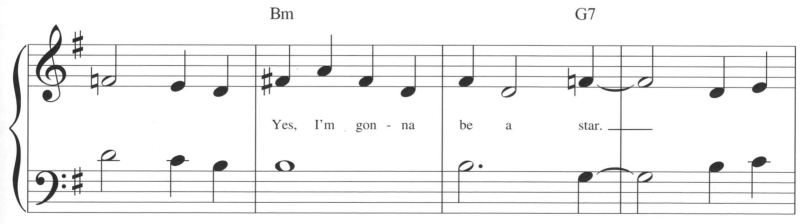

EIGHT DAYS A WEEK

Words and Music by JOHN LENNON
and PAUL McCARTNEY

Eight days a week I love _____ you. ___

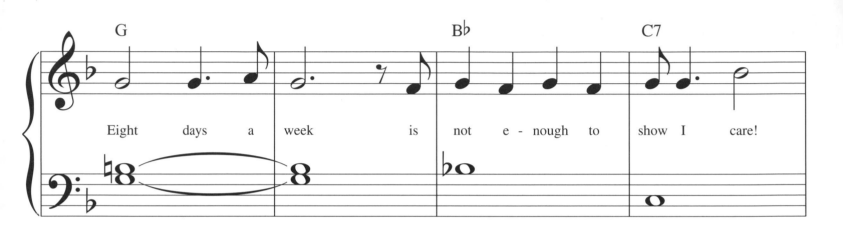

Eight days a week is not e - nough to show I care!

Ooh, I need your love, babe, ___ guess you know it's true;
Love you ev - 'ry day, girl, ___ al - ways on my mind;

hope you need my love, babe ___ just like I need you.
one thing I can say, girl, ___ love you all the time.

Hold me, ____ love me, ____ hold me, ____ love me, ____ I

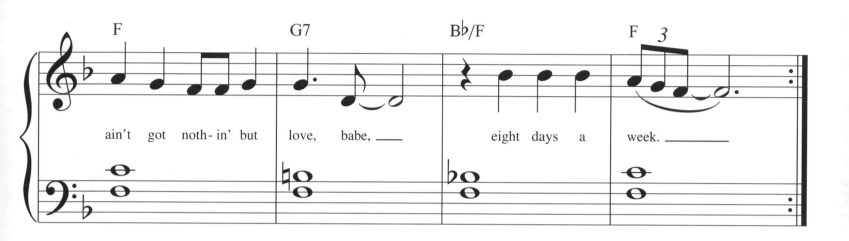

ain't got noth-in' but love, babe, ____ eight days a week. ____

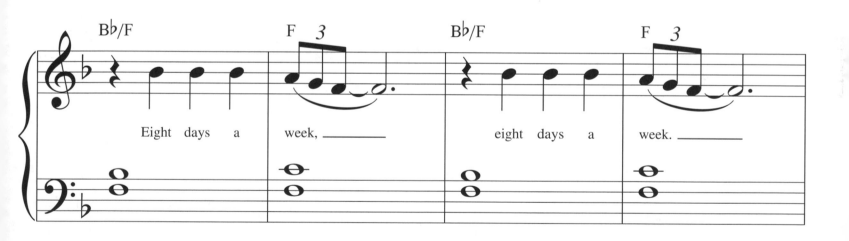

Eight days a week, ____ eight days a week. ____

ELEANOR RIGBY

Words and Music by JOHN LENNON
and PAUL McCARTNEY

Moderately, with a steady beat

Ah, _____ look at all _____ the lone - ly

peo - ple!

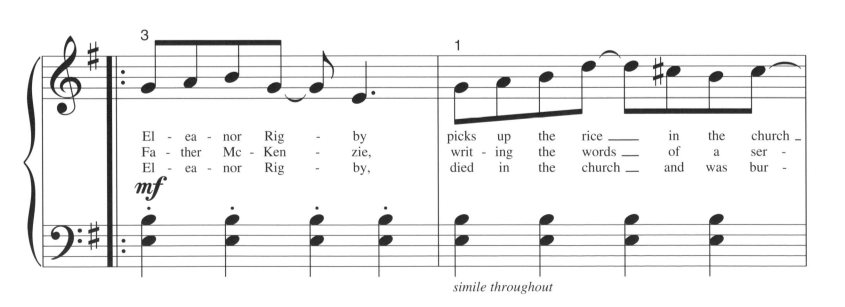

El - ea - nor Rig - by   picks up the rice _____ in the church _____
Fa - ther Mc - Ken - zie,   writ - ing the words _____ of a ser -
El - ea - nor Rig - by,   died in the church _____ and was bur -

simile throughout

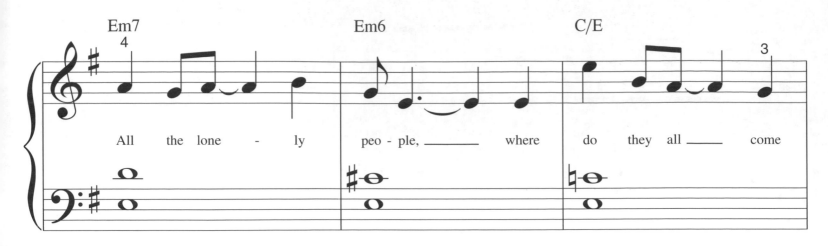

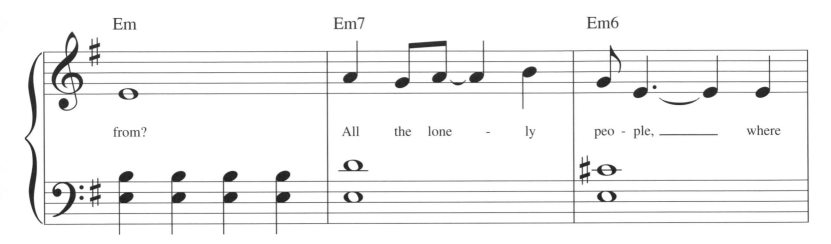

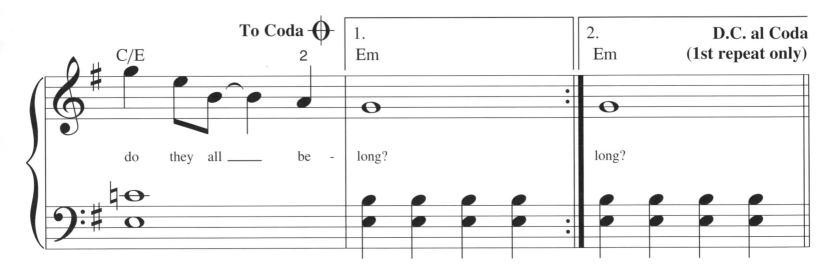

THE FOOL ON THE HILL

Words and Music by JOHN LENNON
and PAUL McCARTNEY

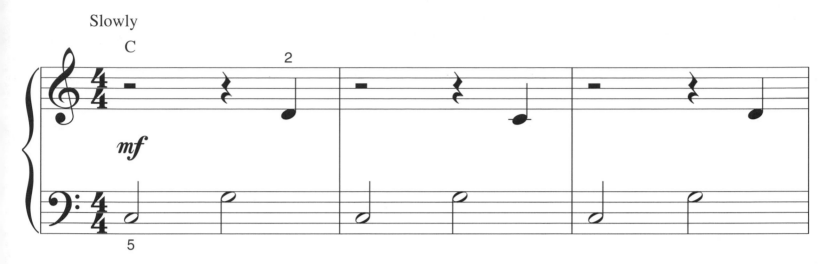

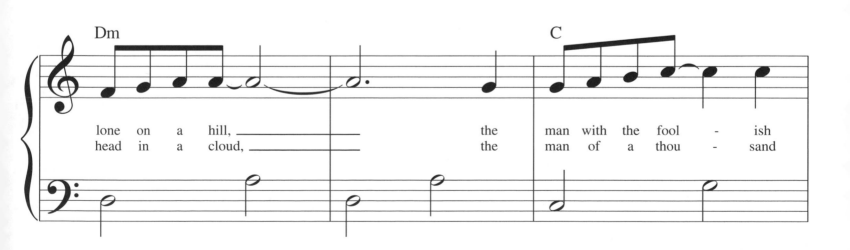

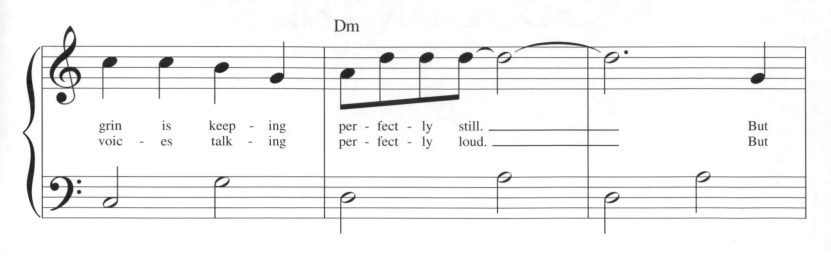

grin is keep - ing per - fect - ly still. _____ But
voic - es talk - ing per - fect - ly loud. _____ But

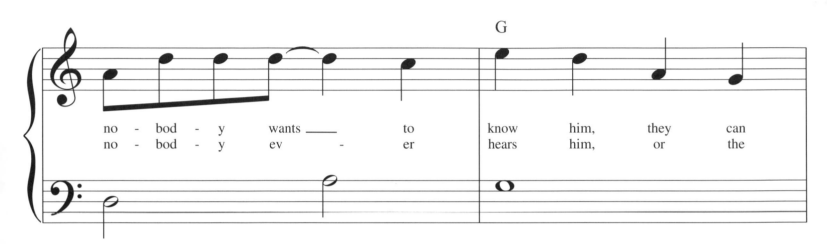

no - bod - y wants _____ to know him, they can
no - bod - y ev - er hears him, or can the

see that he's just _____ a fool. _____ And
sound he ap - pears _____ to make. _____ And

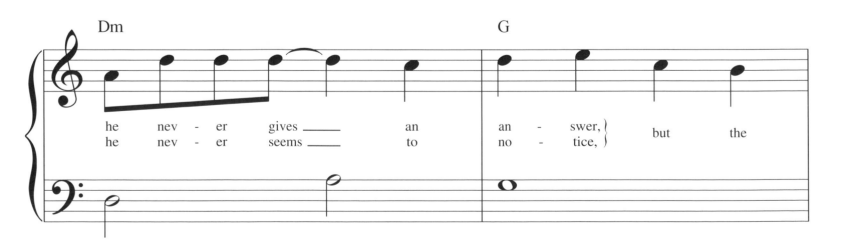

he nev - er gives _____ an an - swer, { but the
he nev - er seems _____ to no - tice, }

FROM ME TO YOU

Words and Music by JOHN LENNON
and PAUL McCARTNEY

keep you by my side, I've got lips that long to

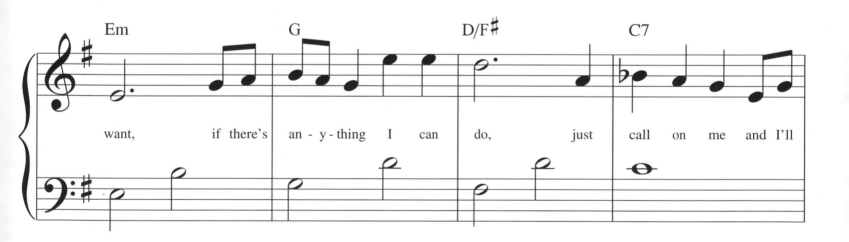

kiss ___ you and keep you sat - is - fied. If there's an - y-thing that you

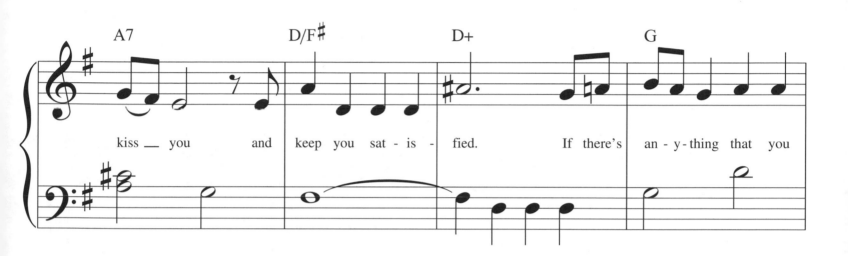

want, if there's an - y-thing I can do, just call on me and I'll

send it a - long ___ with love from me ___ to you.

GET BACK

Words and Music by JOHN LENNON
and PAUL McCARTNEY

GOLDEN SLUMBERS

Words and Music by JOHN LENNON
and PAUL McCARTNEY

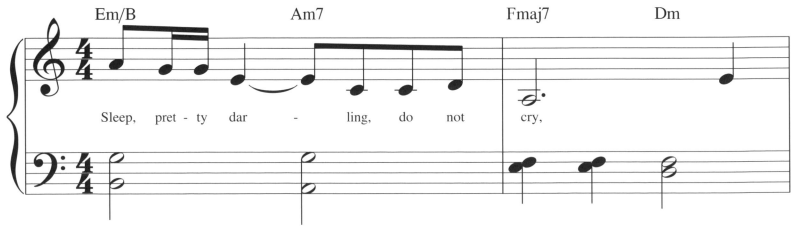

GOOD DAY SUNSHINE

Words and Music by JOHN LENNON
and PAUL McCARTNEY

sun is out,
shad - y tree,

I've got some - thing I can
I love her _____ and she's

laugh a - bout. _____ I feel
lov - ing me. _____ She feels

good
good,

in a
She knows she's

spe - cial way,
look - ing fine,

I'm in love, and it's a
I'm so proud to know that

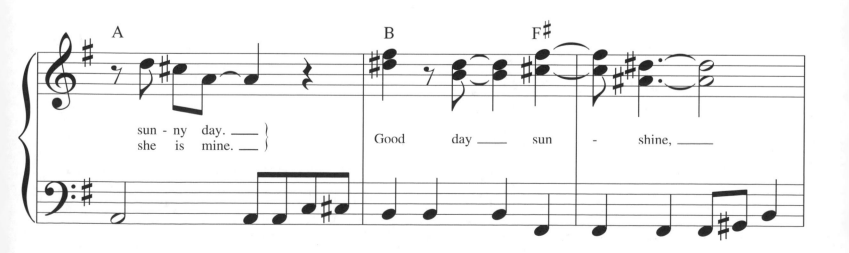

sun - ny day. ___ }
she is mine. ___ }

Good day ___ sun - shine, _____

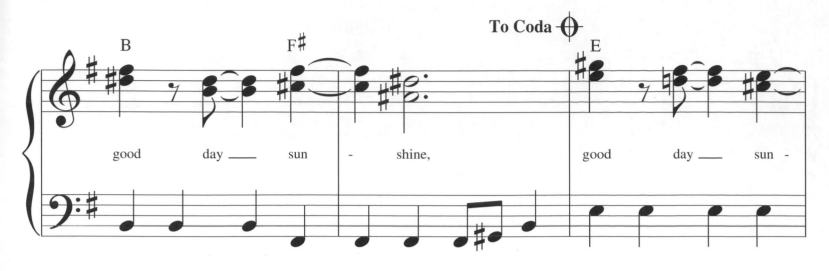

good day _____ sun - shine,   good day _____ sun -

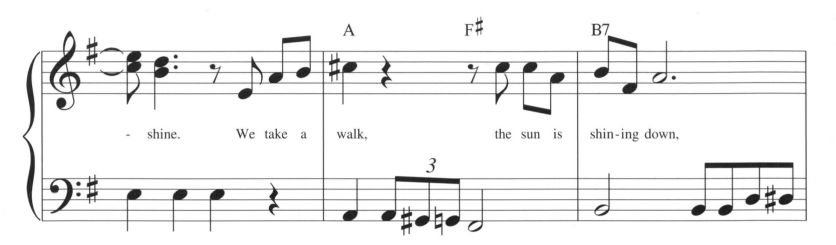

- shine.   We take a   walk,   the sun is   shin-ing down,

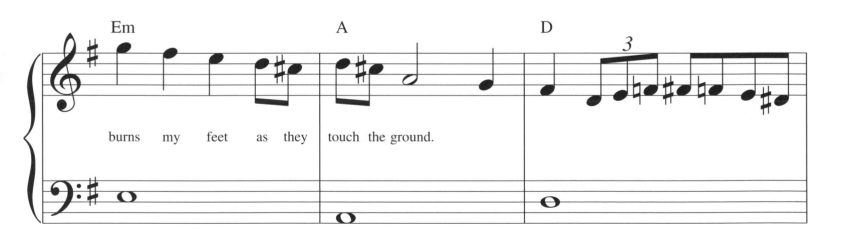

burns my feet as they   touch the ground.

GOOD NIGHT

Words and Music by JOHN LENNON
and PAUL McCARTNEY

Slowly and dreamily

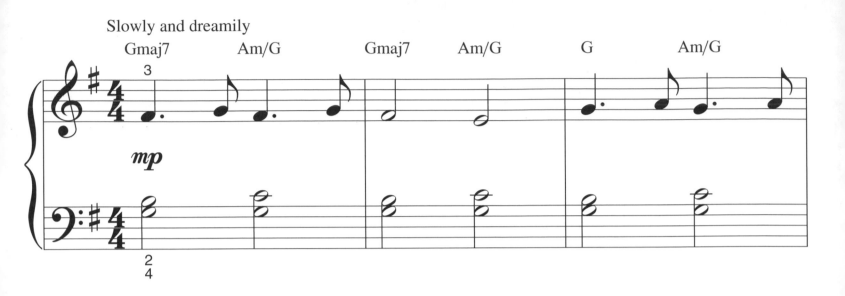

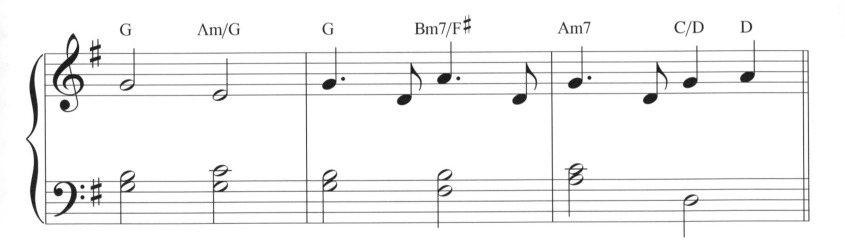

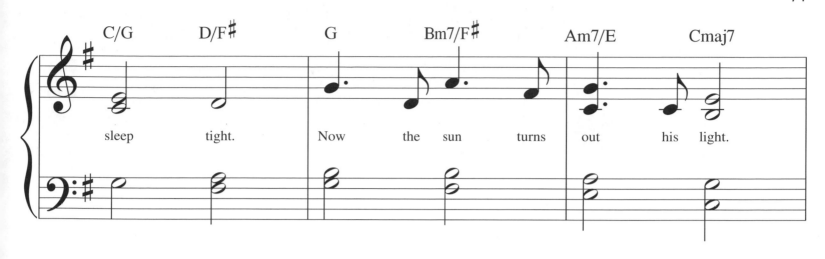

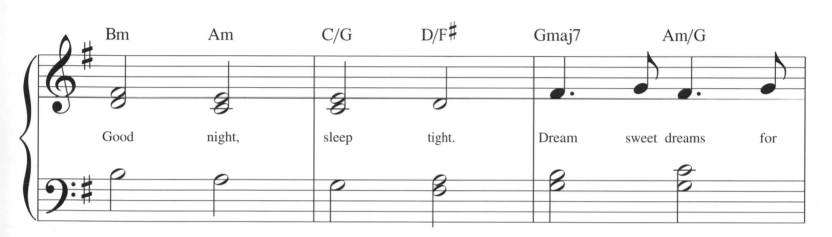

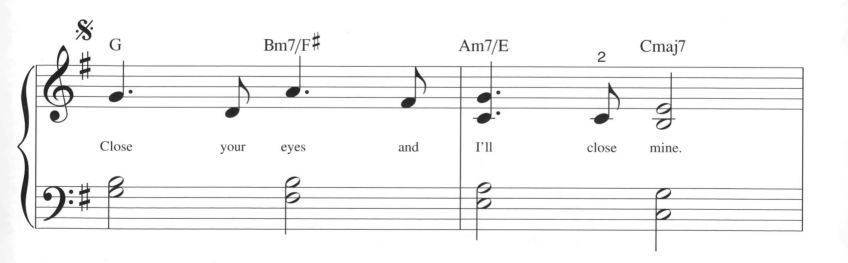

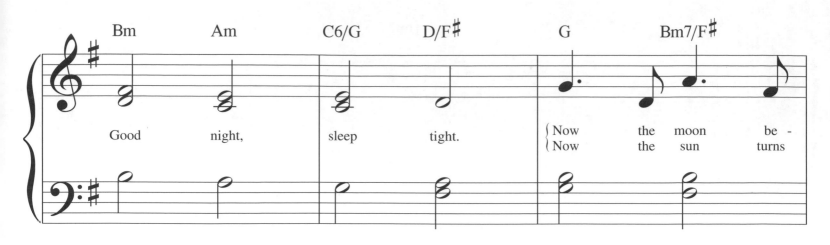

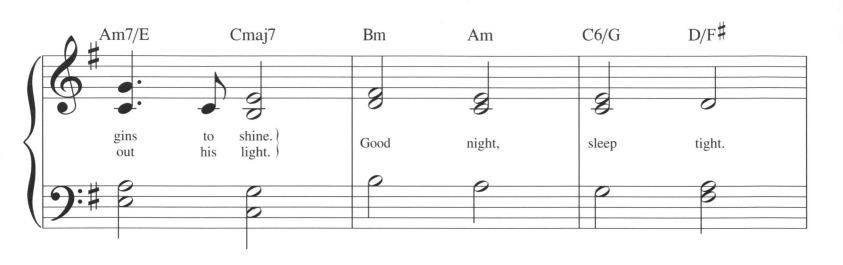

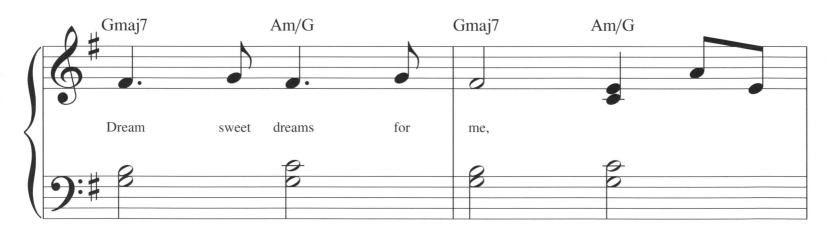

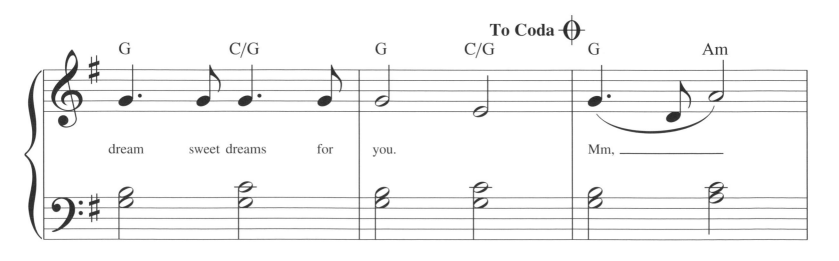

A HARD DAY'S NIGHT

Words and Music by JOHN LENNON
and PAUL McCARTNEY

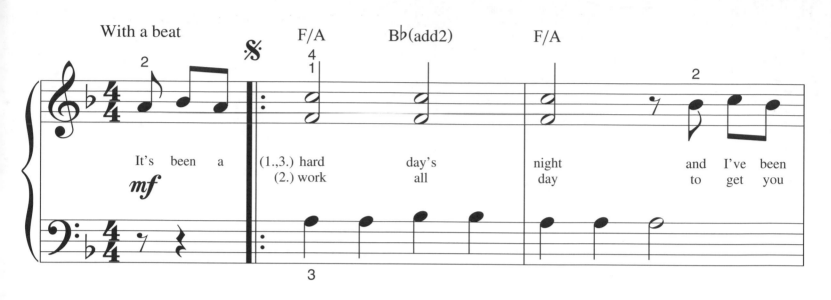

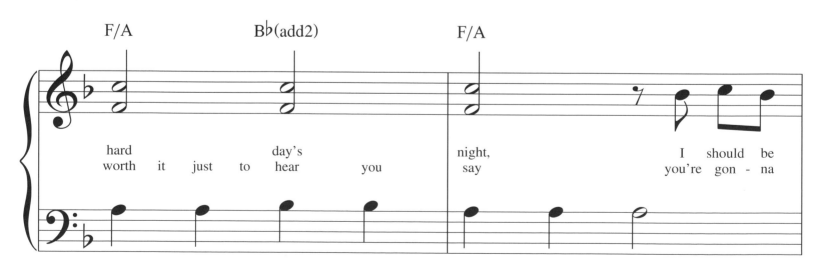

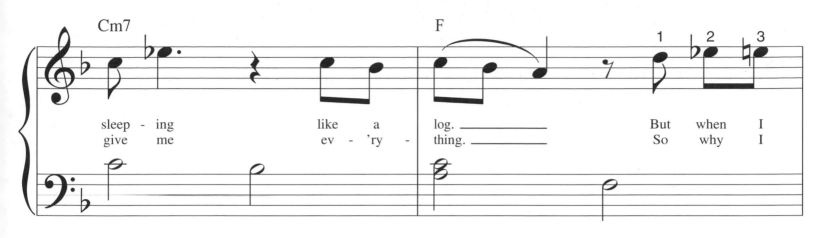

sleep - ing   like   a   log. _____   But   when   I
give   me   ev - 'ry -   thing. _____   So   why   I

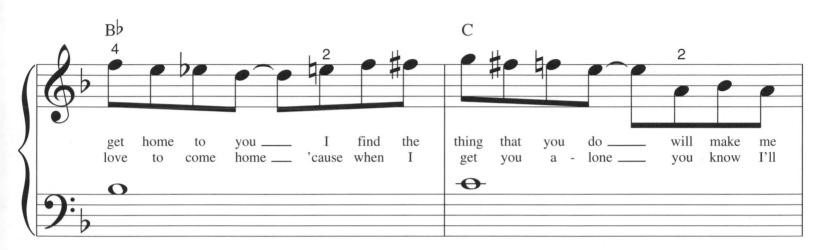

get   home   to   you ____   I   find   the   thing   that   you   do ____   will   make   me
love   to   come   home ____ 'cause   when   I   get   you   a - lone ____   you   know   I'll

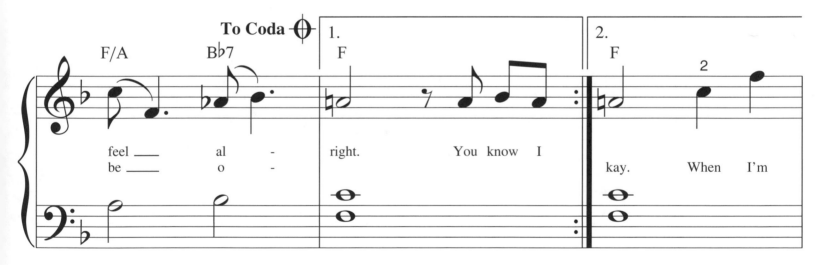

feel ___   al -   right.   You   know   I
be ___   o -   kay.   When   I'm

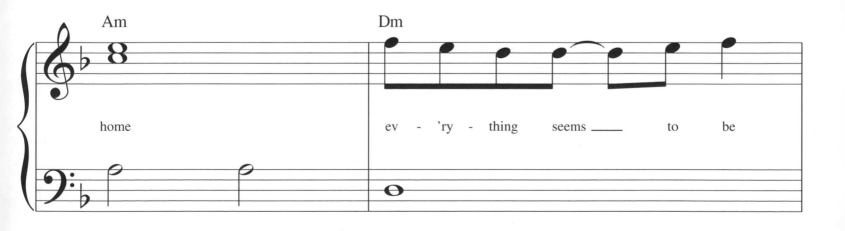

home   ev - 'ry - thing   seems ____   to   be

al - right, when I'm home

D.S. al Coda

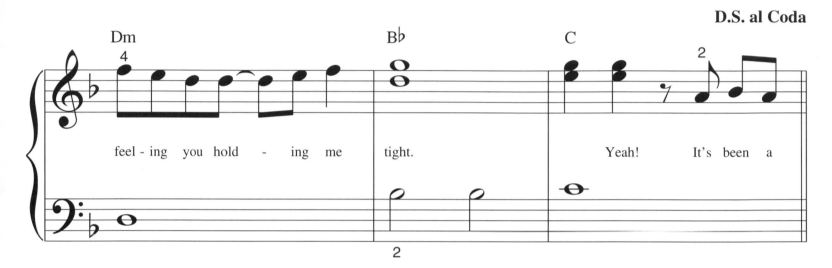

feel-ing you hold - ing me tight. Yeah! It's been a

CODA

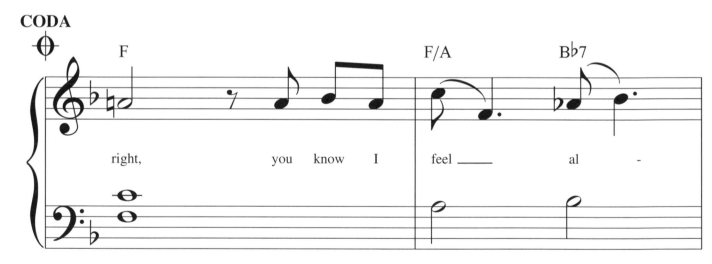

right, you know I feel _____ al -

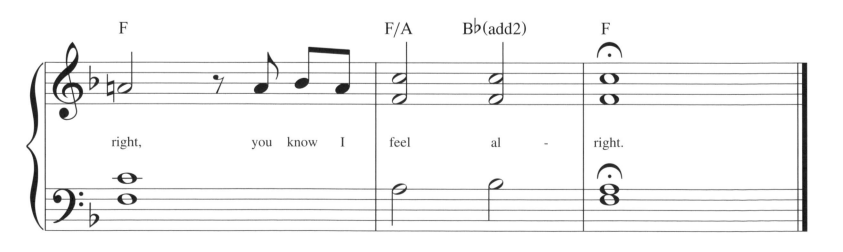

right, you know I feel al - right.

GOT TO GET YOU INTO MY LIFE

Words and Music by JOHN LENNON
and PAUL McCARTNEY

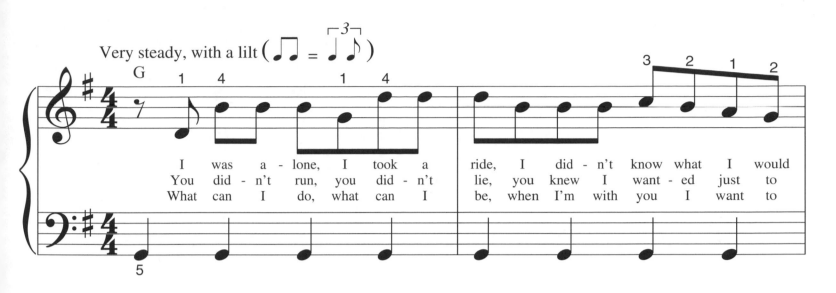

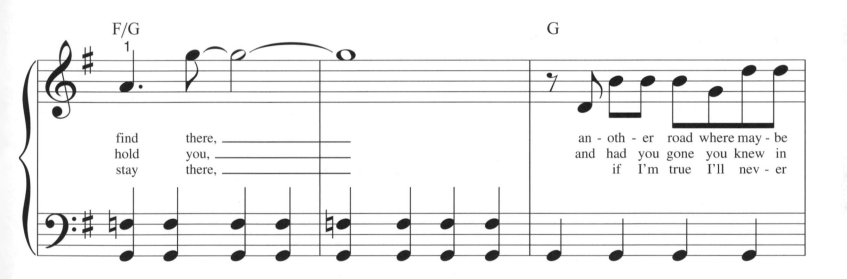

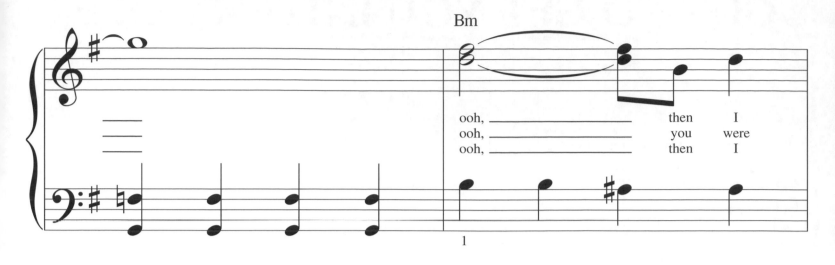

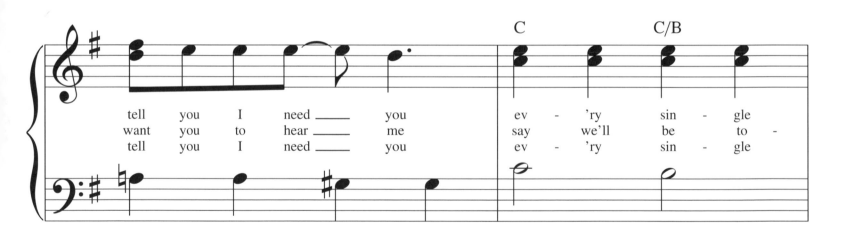

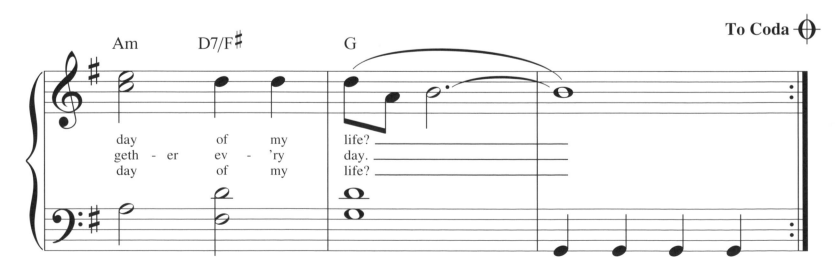

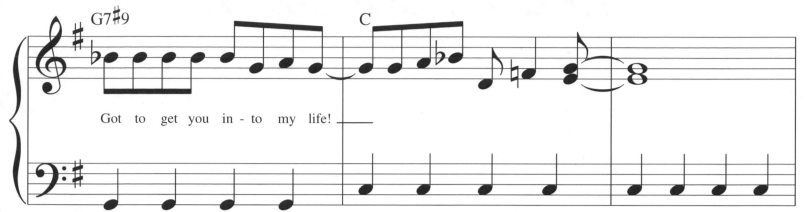

**D.C. al Coda
(no repeat)**

CODA

Got to get you in - to my life!

HELLO, GOODBYE

Words and Music by JOHN LENNON
and PAUL McCARTNEY

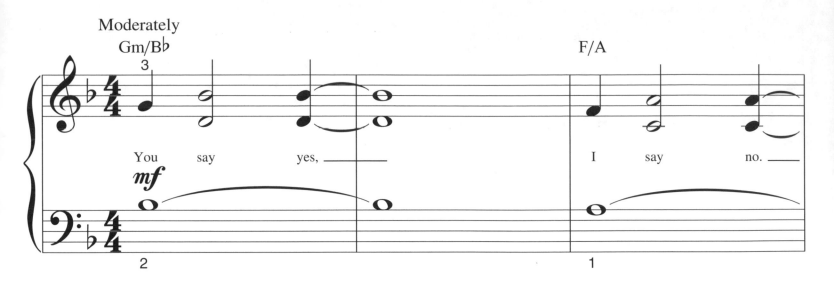

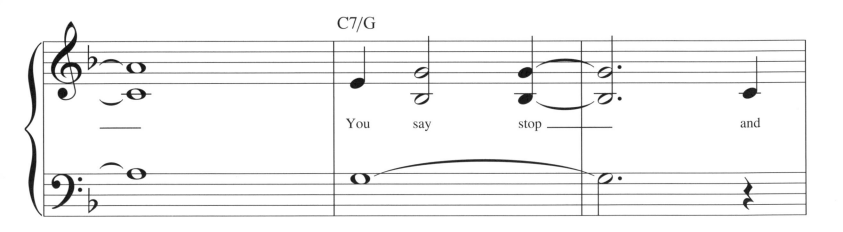

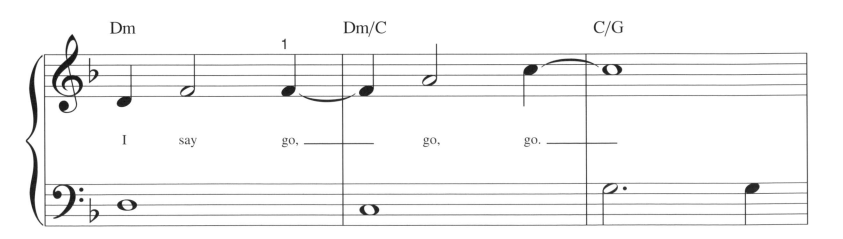

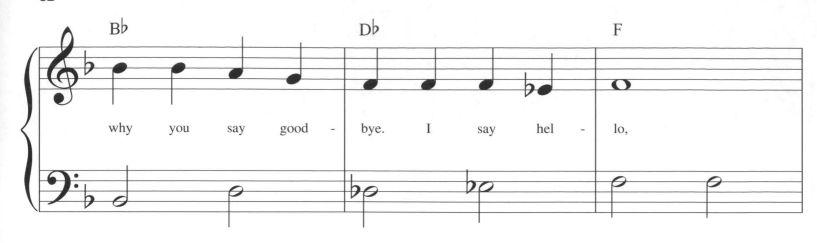

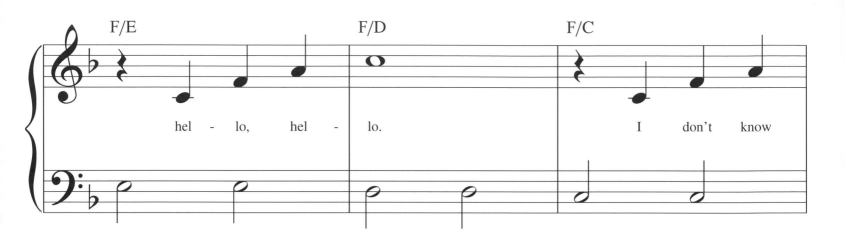

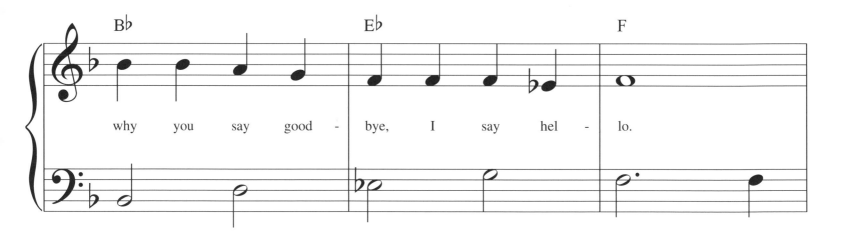

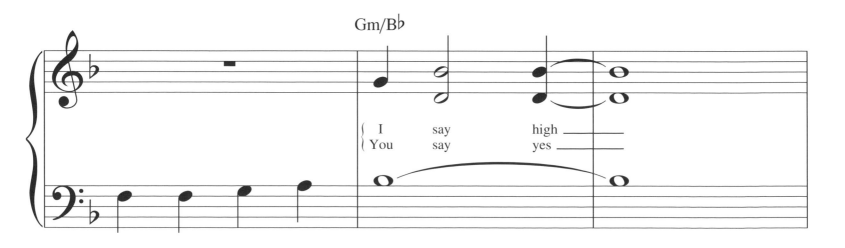

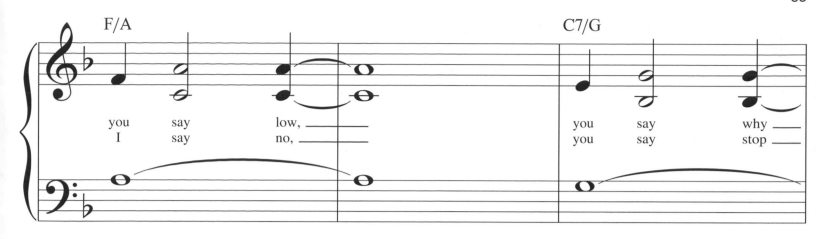

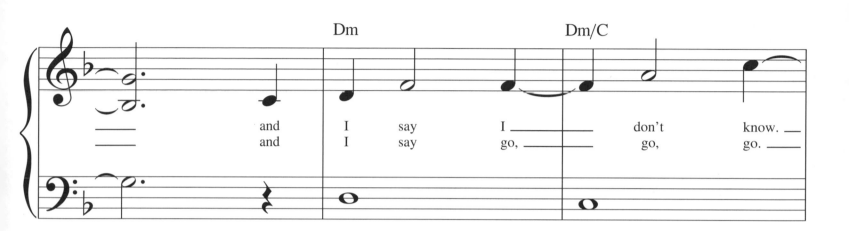

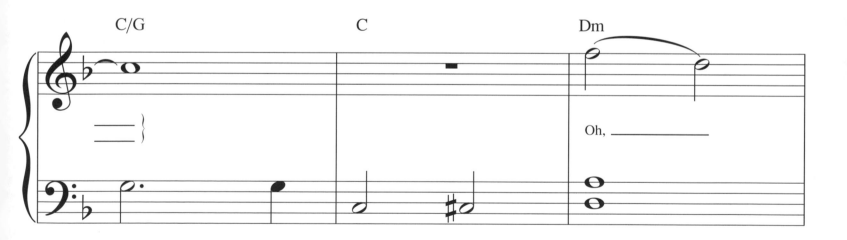

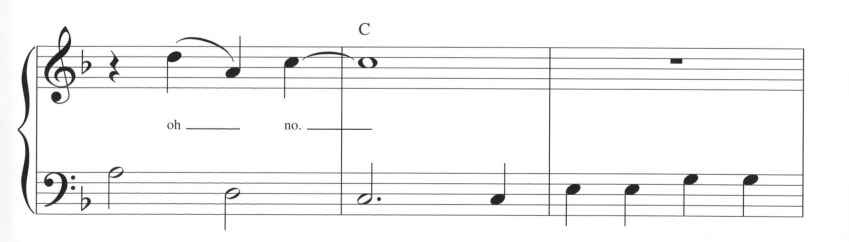

You say _____ good - bye _____ and

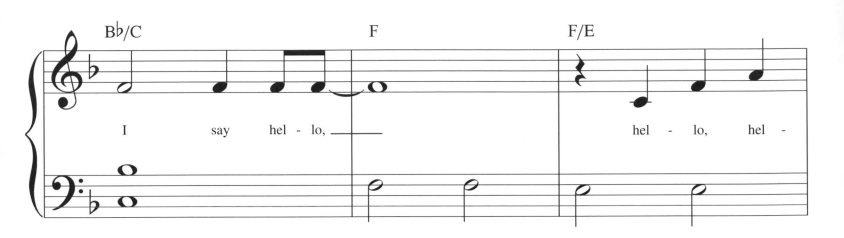

I say hel - lo, _____ hel - lo, hel -

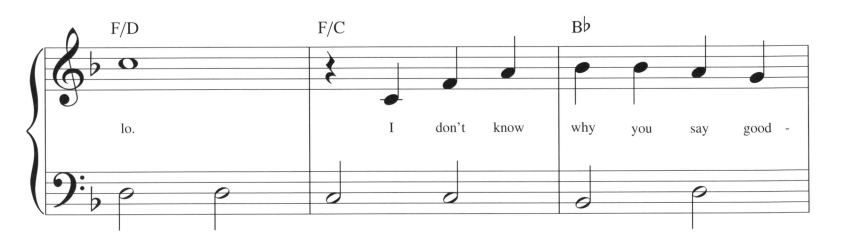

lo. I don't know why you say good -

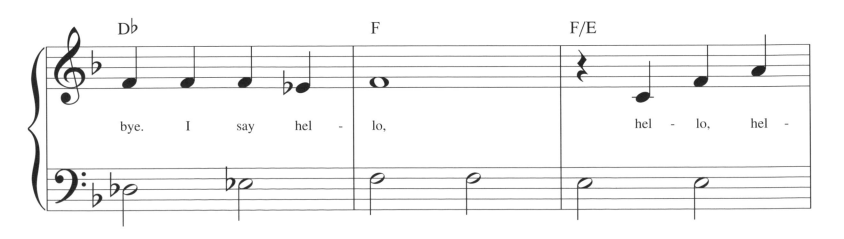

bye. I say hel - lo, hel - lo, hel -

85

lo.   I don't know   why you say good-

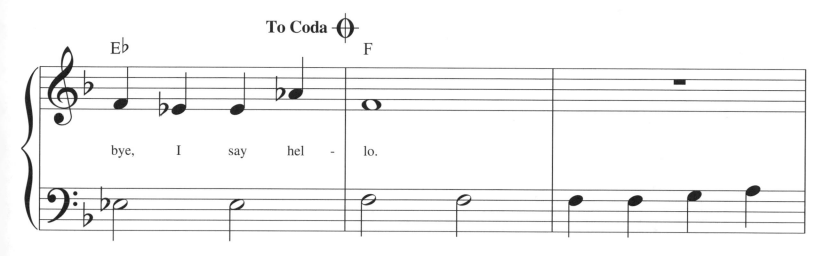

bye, I say hel - lo.

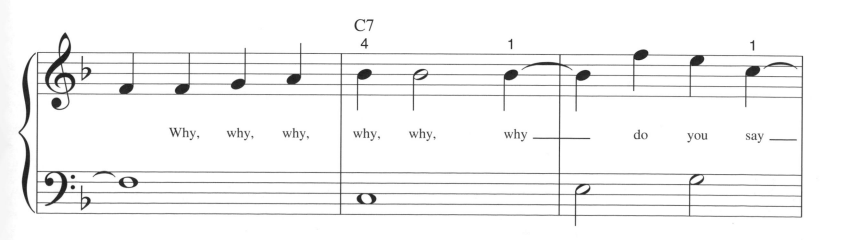

Why, why, why, why, why, why ____ do you say ____

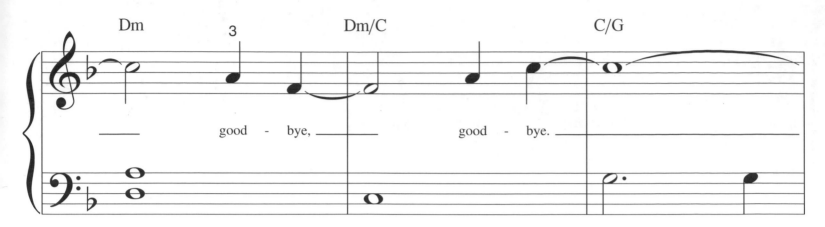

good - bye, ____ good - bye. ____

D.S. al Coda

____

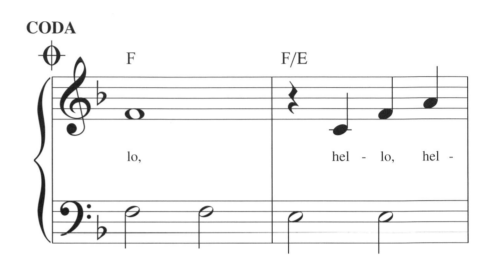

CODA

lo, hel - lo, hel -

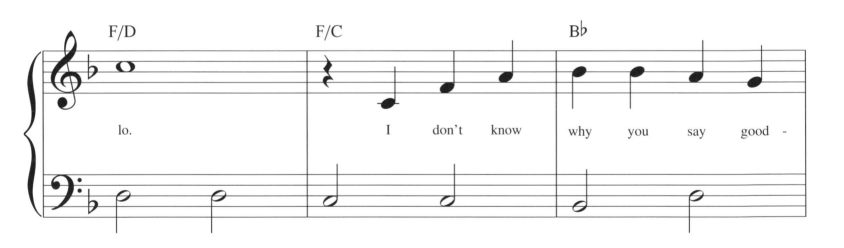

lo. I don't know why you say good -

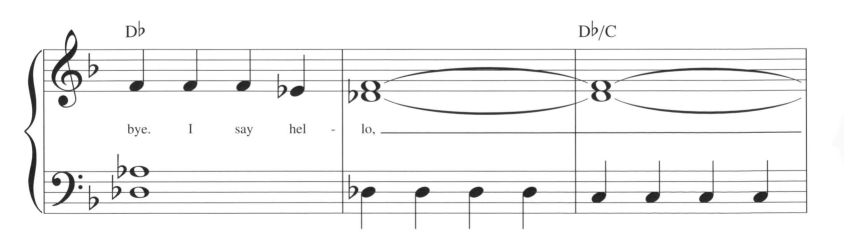

bye. I say hel - lo, ____

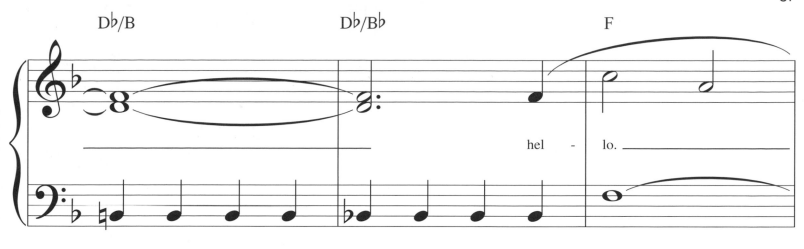

hel - lo. _____

Hey - la _____ he - ba hel -

lo - a, _____ hey - la _____

_____ he - ba hel - lo - a. _____

HELP!

Words and Music by JOHN LENNON
and PAUL McCARTNEY

help in an-y way.
van - ish in the haze.
But now these days are gone, I'm
But ev - 'ry now and then I

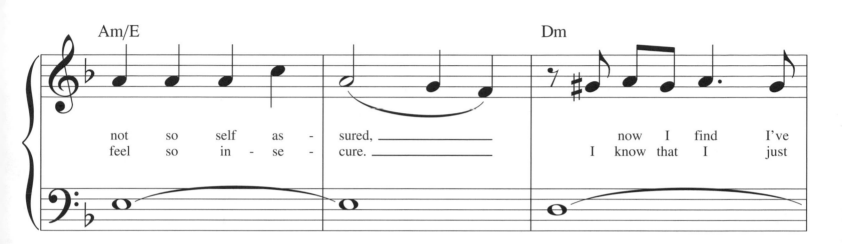

not so self as - sured, _____
feel so in - se - cure. _____
now I find I've
I know that I just

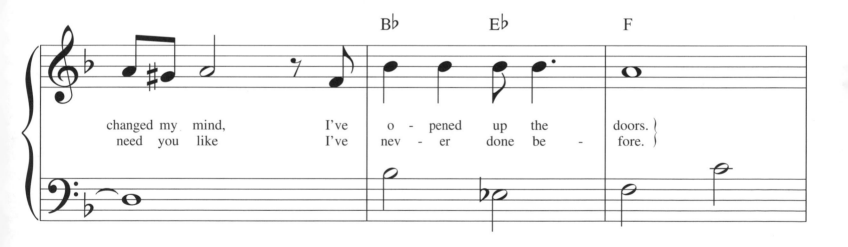

changed my mind, I've o - pened up the doors.
need you like I've nev - er done be - fore.

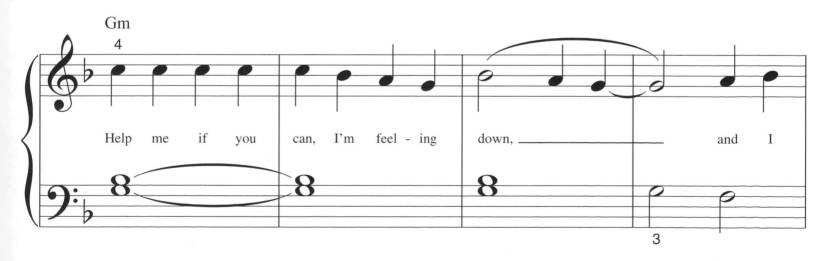

Help me if you can, I'm feel - ing down, _____ and I

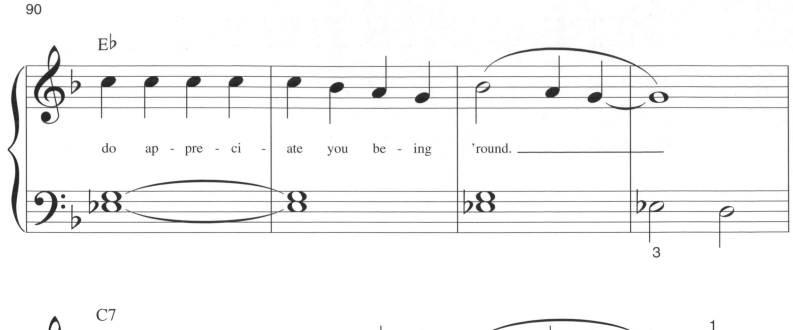

do ap - pre - ci - ate you be - ing 'round.

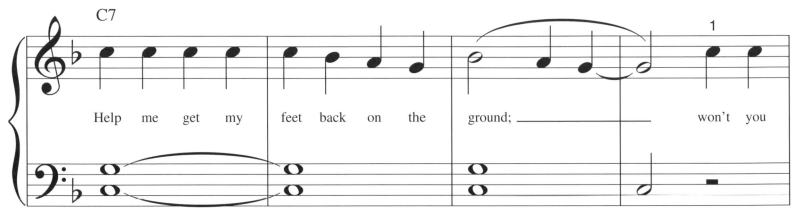

Help me get my feet back on the ground; won't you

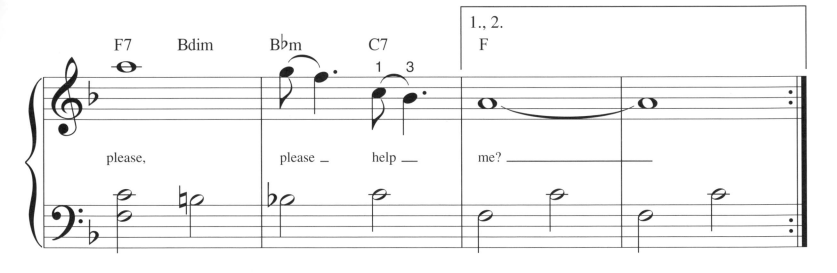

please, please help me?

1., 2.
me?

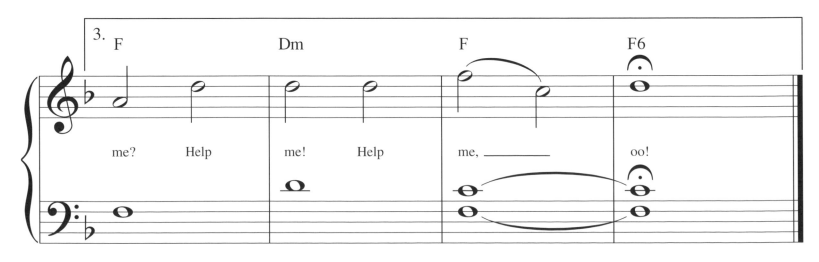

3.
me? Help me! Help me, oo!

HERE COMES THE SUN

Words and Music by
GEORGE HARRISON

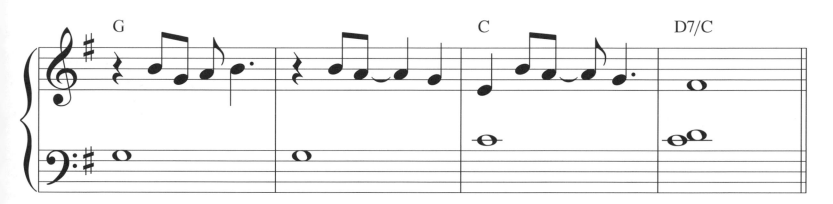

Here comes _ the sun, doo da doo doo. Here comes _ the

sun, And I say, "It's all right."

sun,   and I say,   "It's   all   right."

1., 2.

3.

"It's   all   right."

HERE, THERE AND EVERYWHERE

Words and Music by JOHN LENNON
and PAUL McCARTNEY

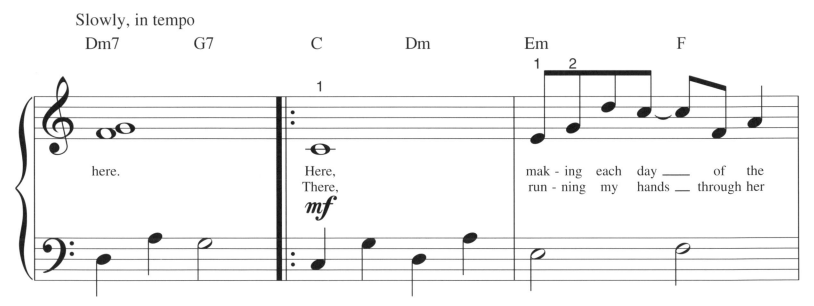

HEY JUDE

Words and Music by JOHN LENNON
and PAUL McCARTNEY

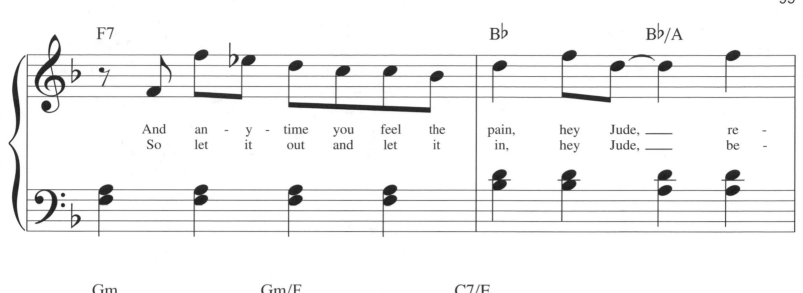

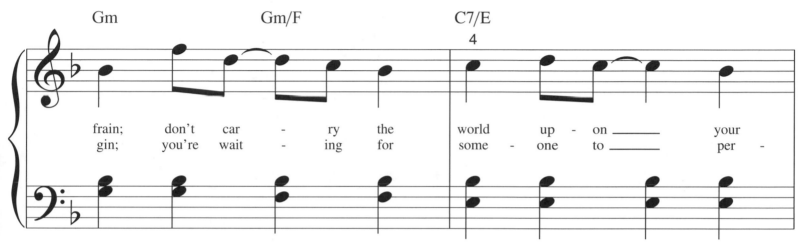

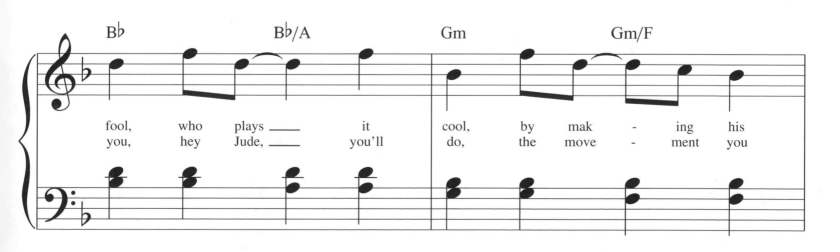

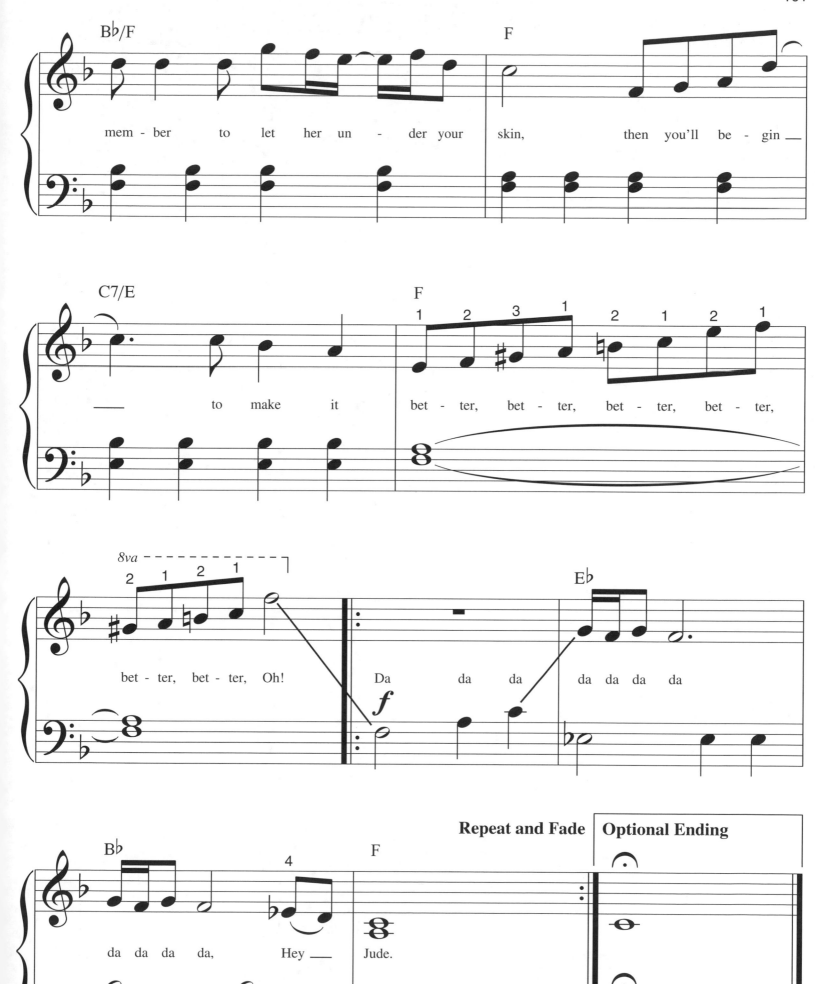

I FEEL FINE

Words and Music by JOHN LENNON
and PAUL McCARTNEY

Bright Rock tempo

Ba - by's good to
Ba - by says she's

me, you know, __ she's
mine, you know, __ she

hap - py as can
tells me all the

be, you know, __ she
time, you know, __ she

104

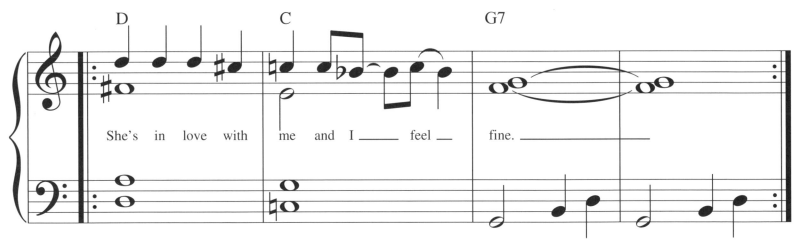

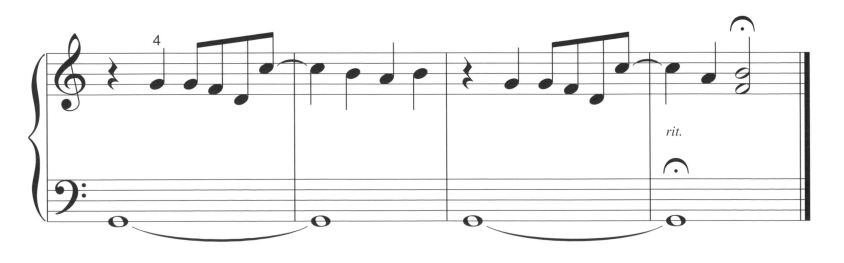

I SAW HER STANDING THERE

Words and Music by JOHN LENNON
and PAUL McCARTNEY

Bright Rock

Well, she was just _____ sev - en - teen, _____ and you
looked at me _____ and

know what I mean, _____ and the way she looked _____ was way _____
I, I could see _____ that be - fore too long _____ I'd fall _____

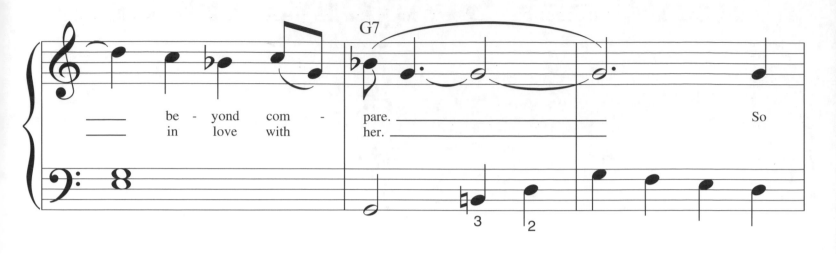

be - yond com - pare. _____ So
in love with her. _____

how could I dance _____ with an - oth - er,
She would-n't dance _____ with an - oth - er,

woo, when I saw her stand - ing
woo, when I saw her stand - ing

there? Well, she _____
there. Well, my

108

held each oth-er tight, ___ and be-fore too long ___ I fell ___

___ in love with her. _____ Now

I'll nev-er dance ___ with an-oth- er,

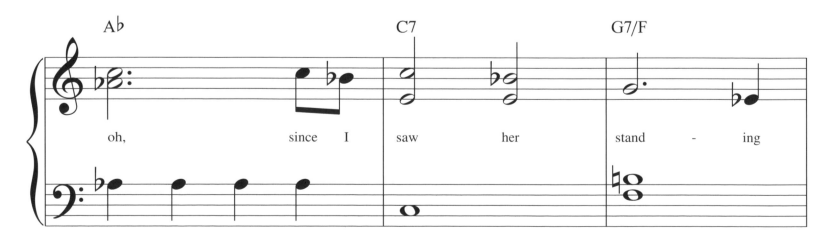

oh, since I saw her stand - ing

I WANT TO HOLD YOUR HAND

Words and Music by JOHN LENNON
and PAUL McCARTNEY

With a steady Rock beat

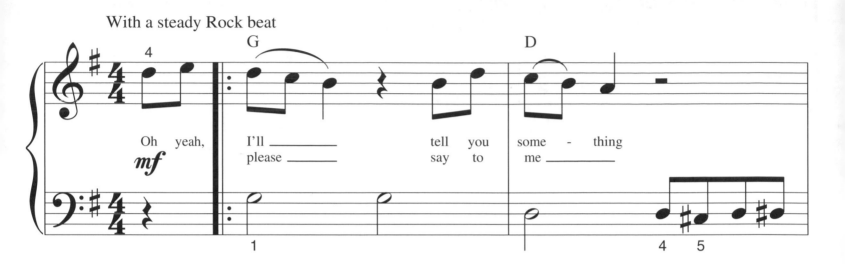

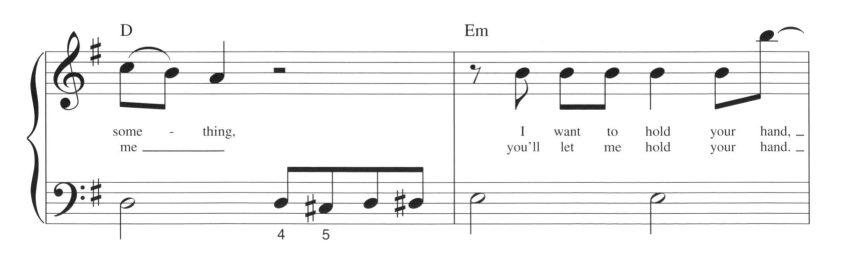

I WILL

Words and Music by JOHN LENNON
and PAUL McCARTNEY

I'LL FOLLOW THE SUN

Words and Music by JOHN LENNON
and PAUL McCARTNEY

Moderately

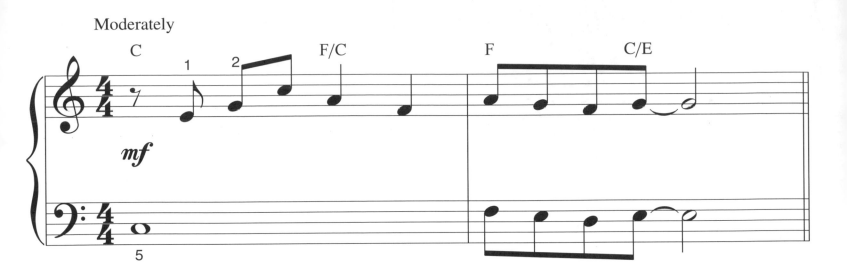

One day ____ you'll look ____ to see I've gone, ____
Some day ____ you'll know ____ I was the one, ____

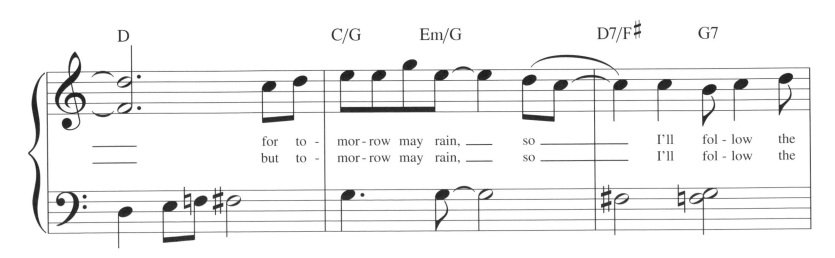

for to- mor-row may rain, ____ so ____ I'll fol-low the
but to- mor-row may rain, ____ so ____ I'll fol-low the

LUCY IN THE SKY
WITH DIAMONDS

Words and Music by JOHN LENNON
and PAUL McCARTNEY

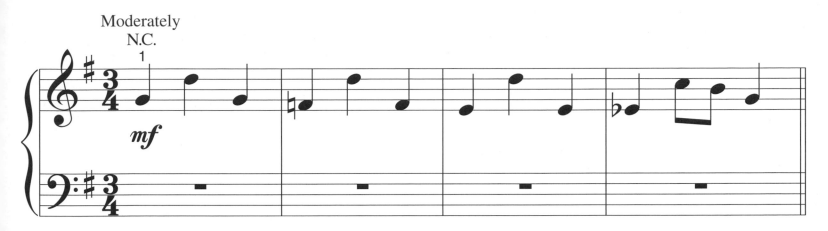

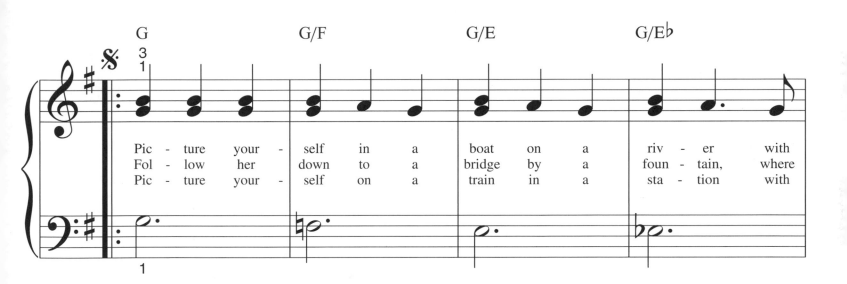

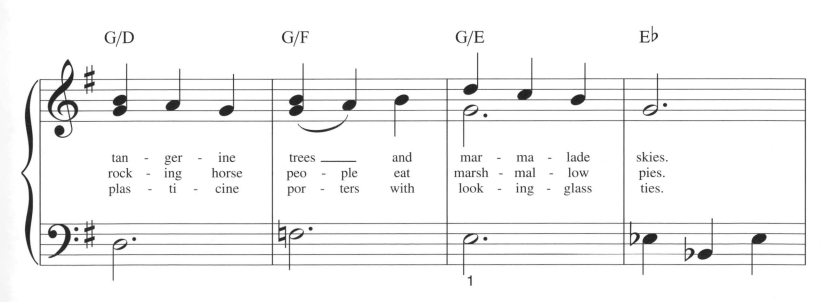

Lu - cy in the sky _____ with dia - monds,

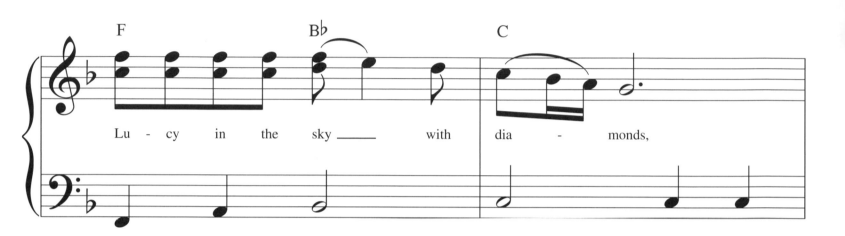

Lu - cy in the sky _____ with dia - monds,

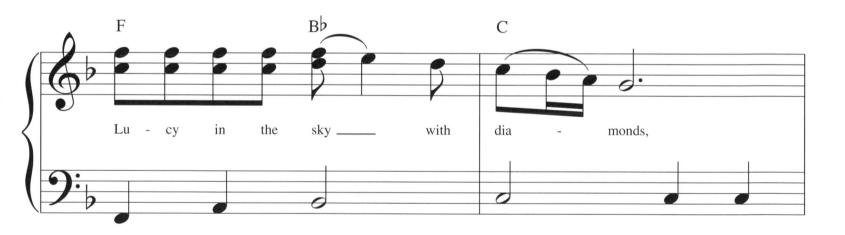

Lu - cy in the sky _____ with dia - monds,

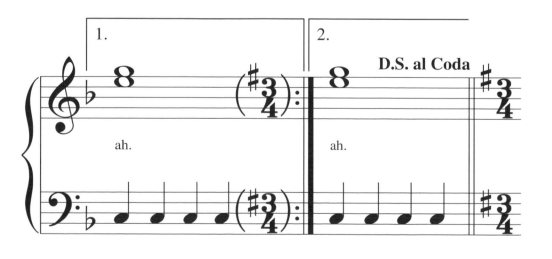

1.

ah.

2.

D.S. al Coda

ah.

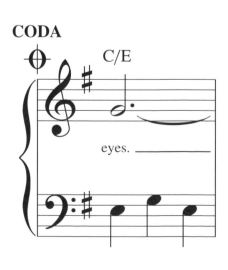

CODA

C/E

eyes. _____

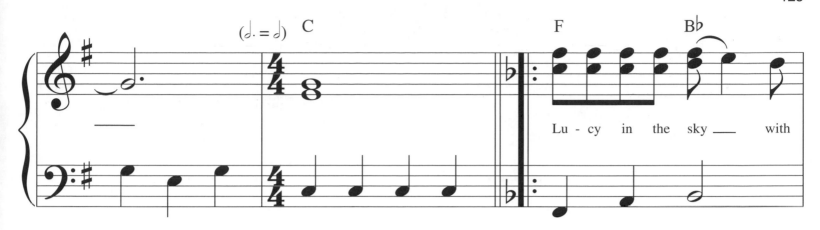

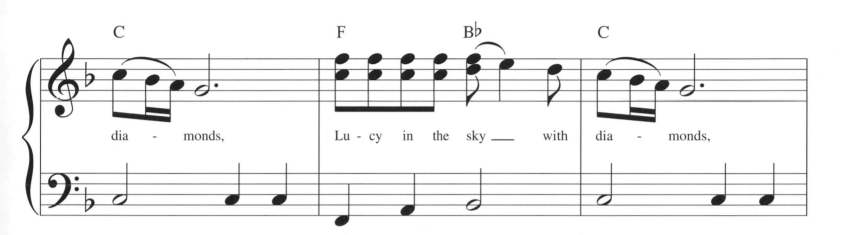

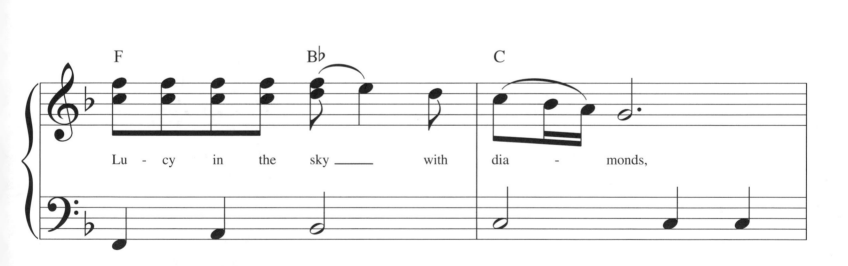

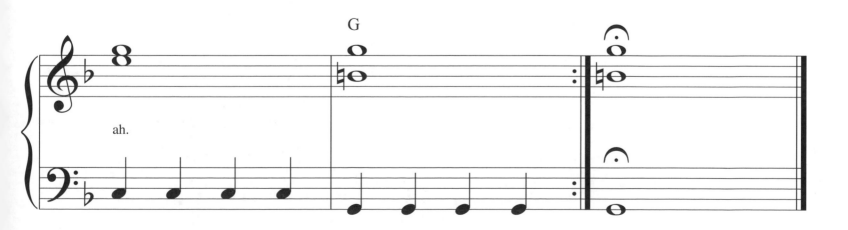

IF I FELL

Words and Music by JOHN LENNON
and PAUL McCARTNEY

Moderately slow, but not dragging

If I fell in love with you, would you prom-ise to be true, and

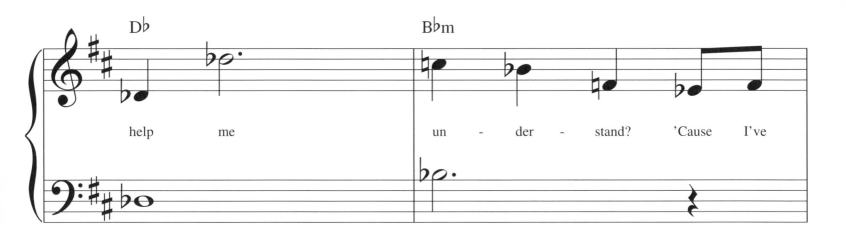

help me un - der - stand? 'Cause I've

been in love be - fore, and I found that love was more than

128

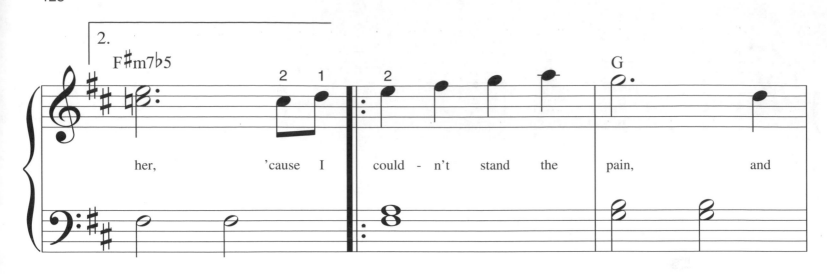

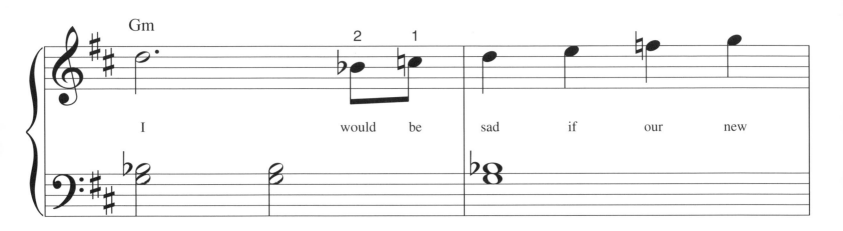

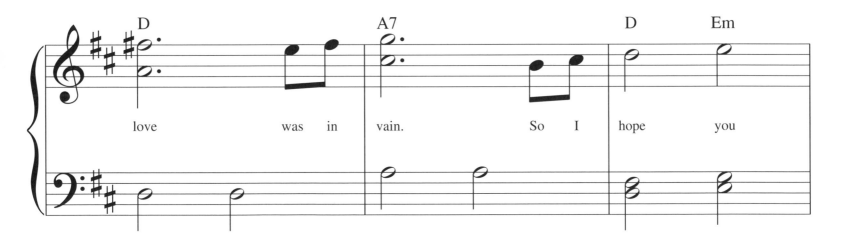

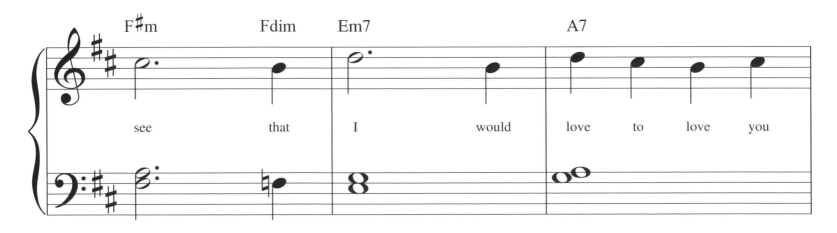

IN MY LIFE

Words and Music by JOHN LENNON
and PAUL McCARTNEY

LADY MADONNA

Words and Music by JOHN LENNON
and PAUL McCARTNEY

Brightly, with a beat

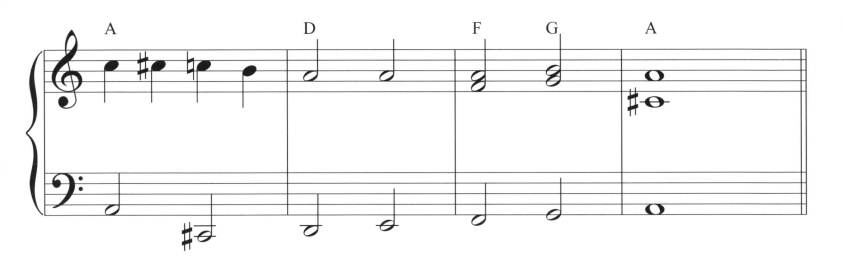

La - dy Ma - don - na,   chil - dren   at   your   feet, ___
La - dy Ma - don - na,   ba - by   at   your   breast, ___
La - dy Ma - don - na,   ly - ing   on   the   bed, ___

134

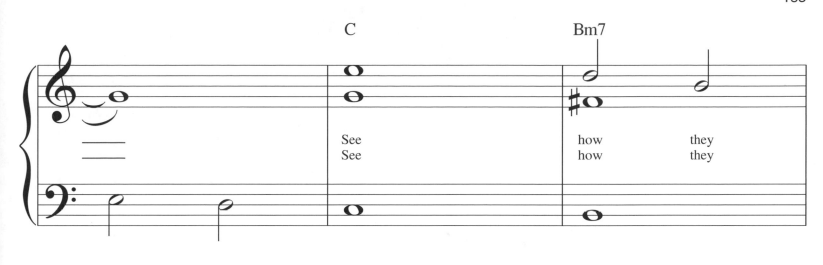

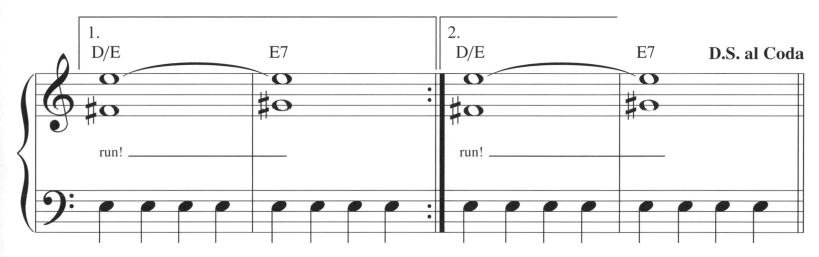

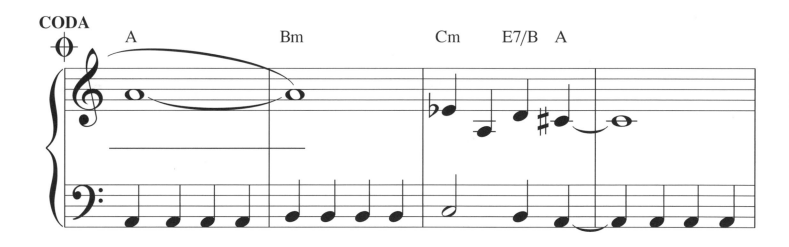

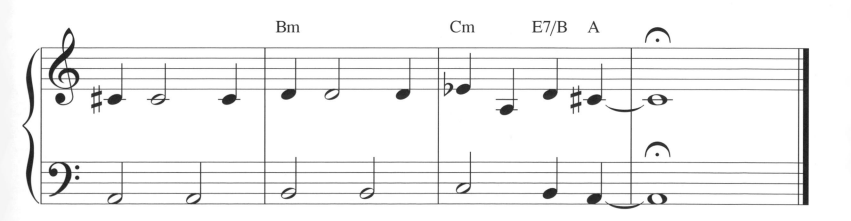

LET IT BE

Words and Music by JOHN LENNON
and PAUL McCARTNEY

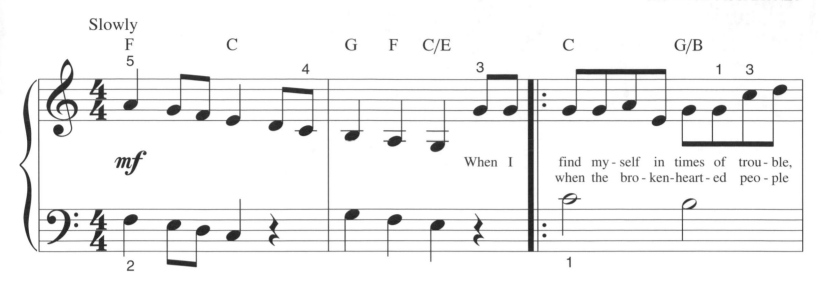

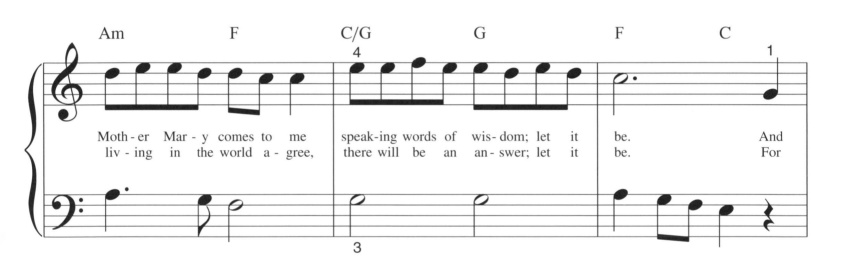

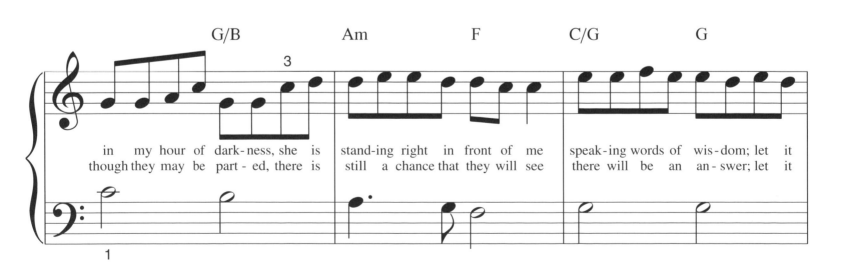

THE LONG AND WINDING ROAD

Words and Music by JOHN LENNON
and PAUL McCARTNEY

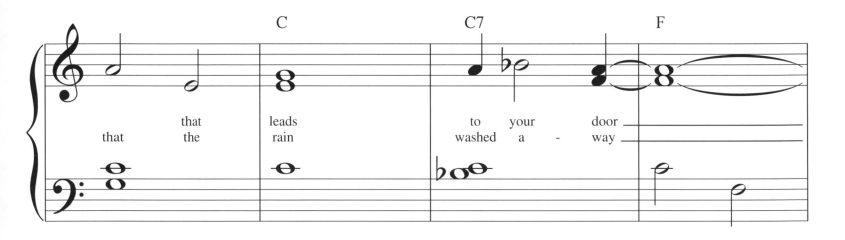

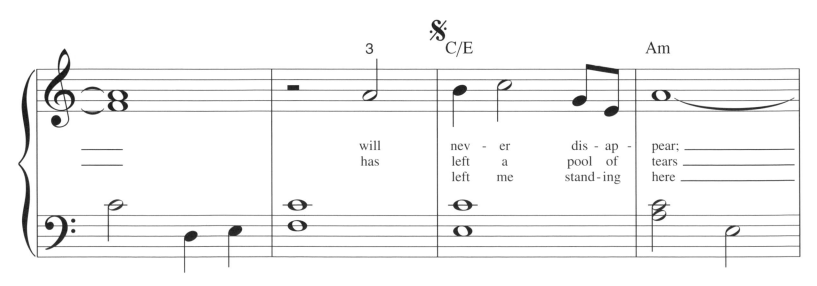

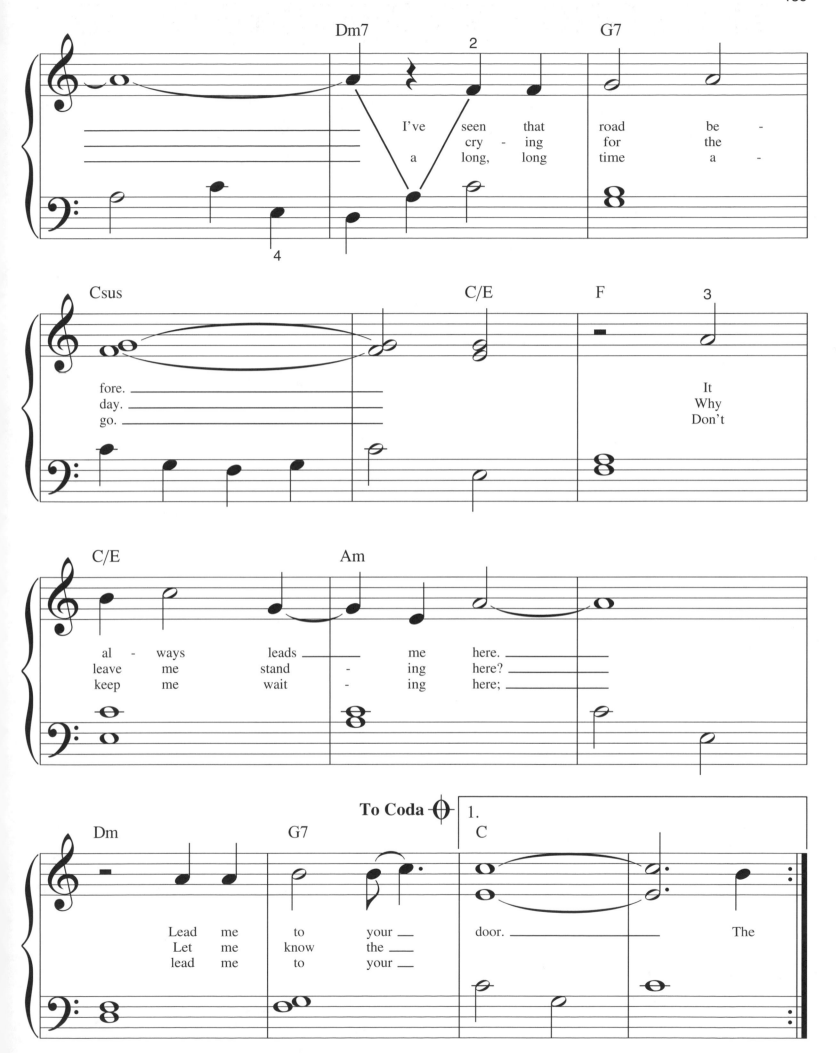

139

140

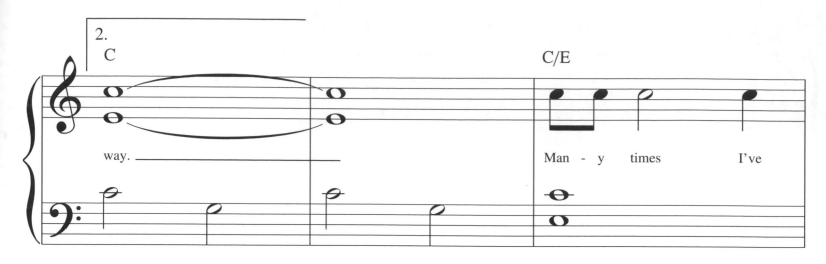

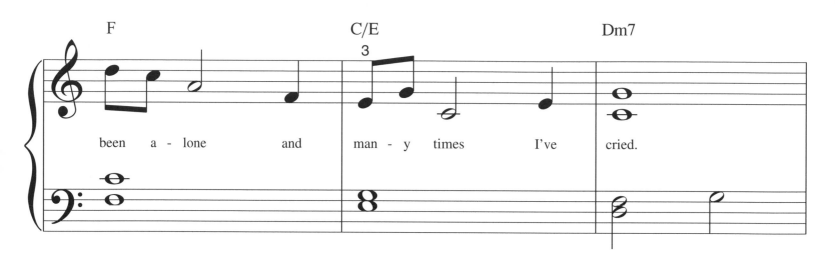

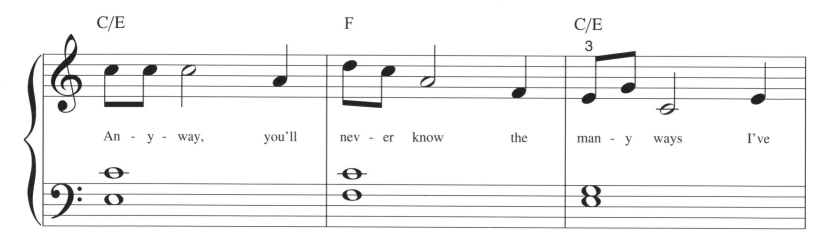

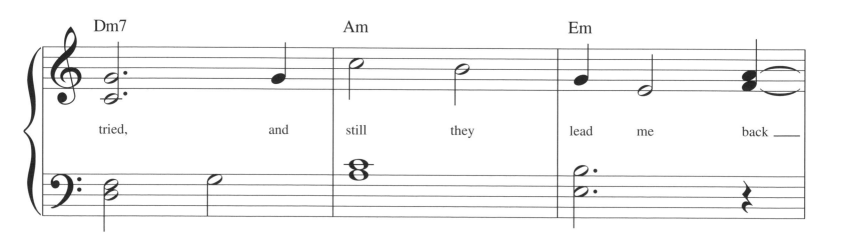

F/G   C

to the   long

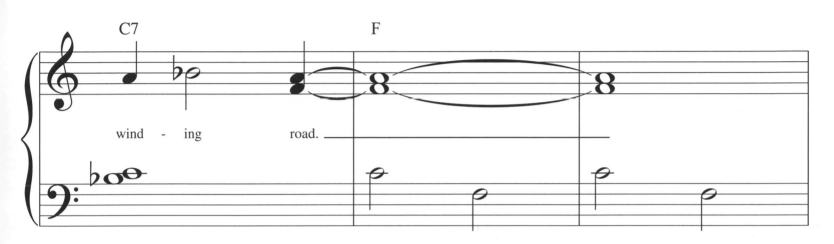

C7   F

wind - ing   road.

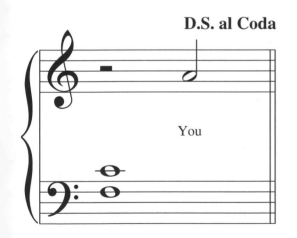

D.S. al Coda

You

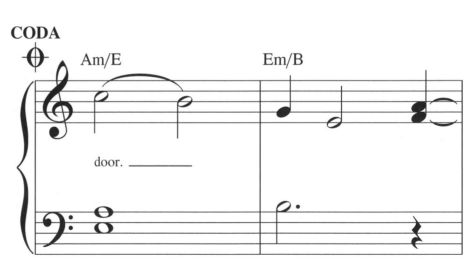

CODA

Am/E   Em/B

door.

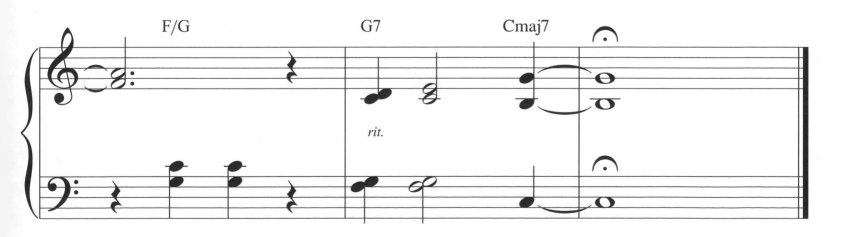

F/G   G7   Cmaj7

rit.

LOVE ME DO

Words and Music by JOHN LENNON
and PAUL McCARTNEY

Moderate Rock

Love, love me do, you know I love

you, I'll al - ways be true, so please

love me do! Whoa,

MAGICAL MYSTERY TOUR

Words and Music by JOHN LENNON
and PAUL McCARTNEY

Fast, with a beat

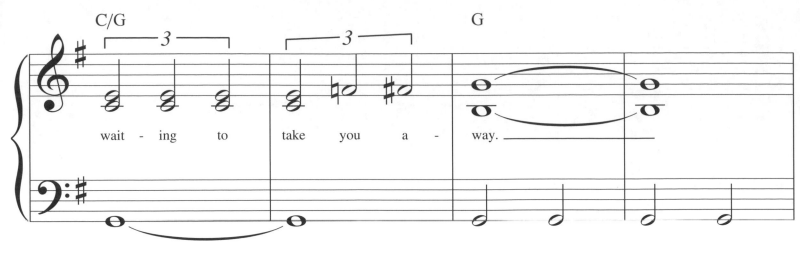

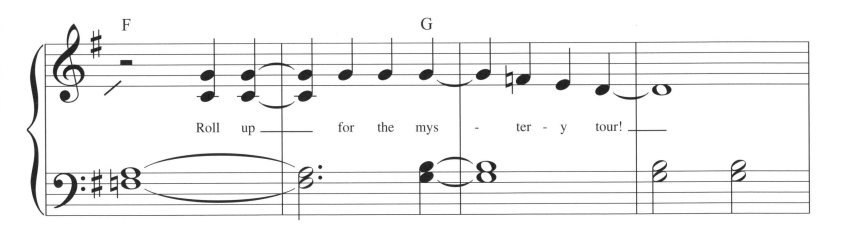

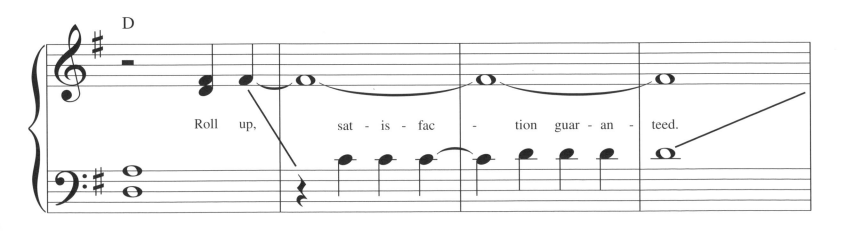

148

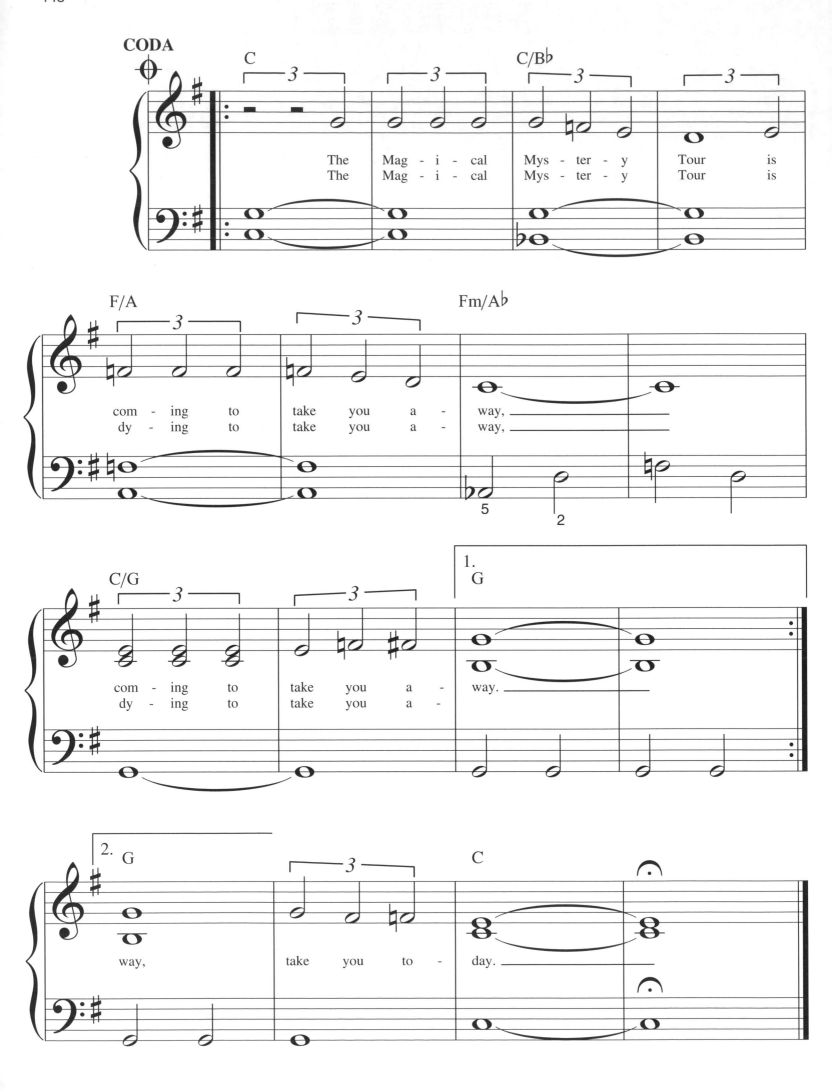

MICHELLE

Words and Music by JOHN LENNON
and PAUL McCARTNEY

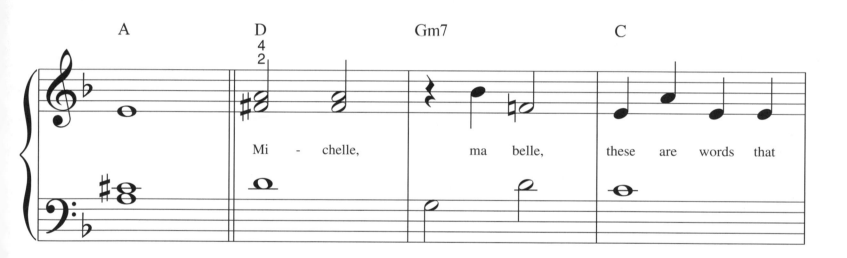

Mi - chelle, ma belle, these are words that

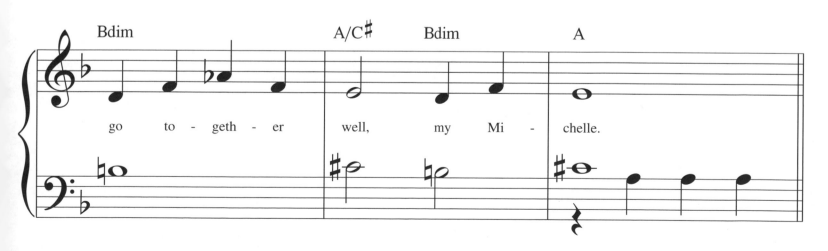

go to - geth - er well, my Mi - chelle.

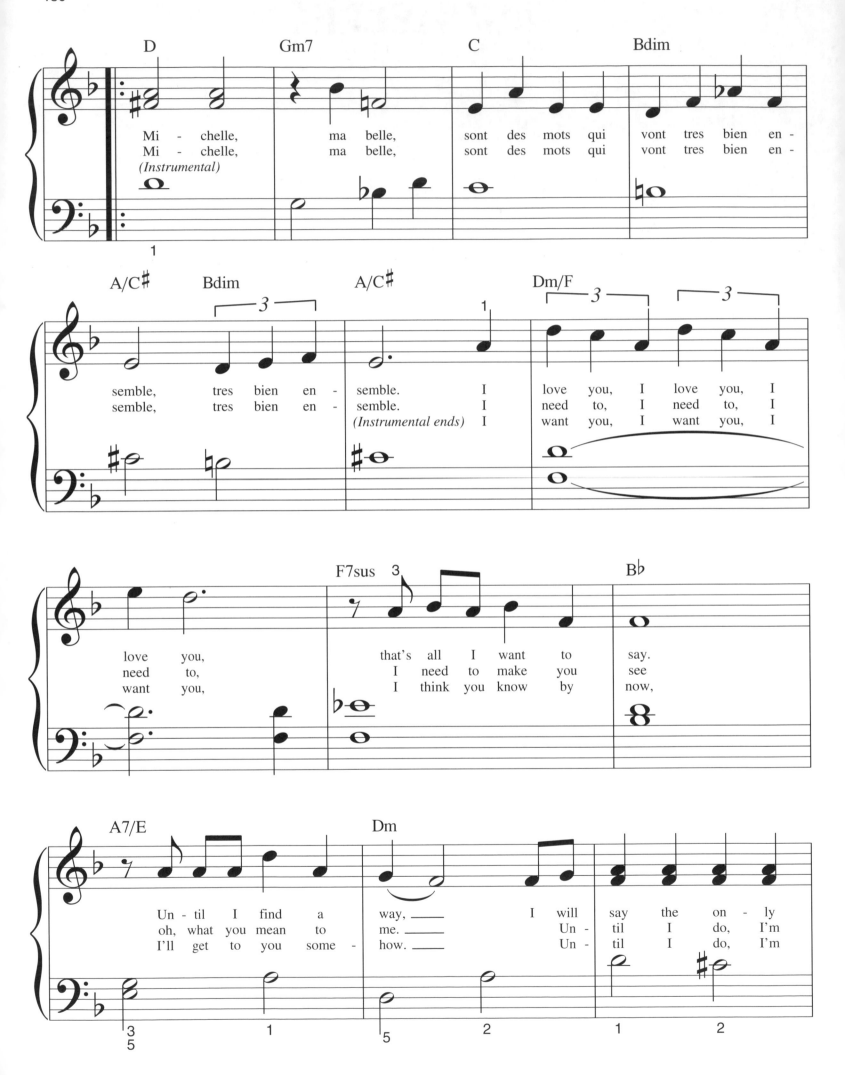

word I know that you'll un - der - stand.
hop - ing you will know what I mean.
tell - ing you so you'll un - der - stand.

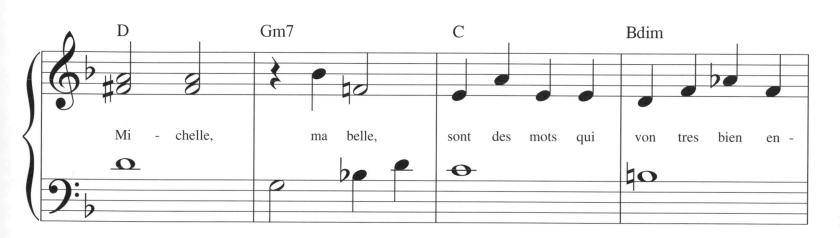

Mi - chelle, ma belle, sont des mots qui von tres bien en -

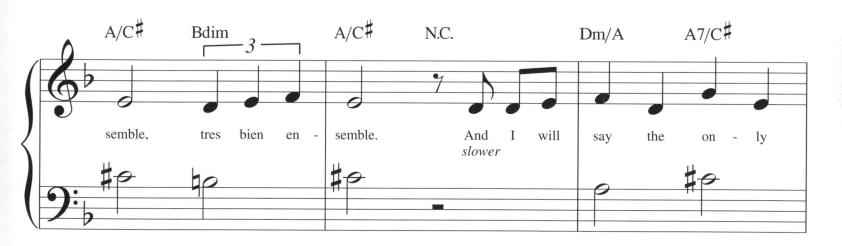

semble, tres bien en - semble. And I will say the on - ly
slower

words I know that you'll un - der - stand, my Mi - chelle.

NOWHERE MAN

Words and Music by JOHN LENNON
and PAUL McCARTNEY

Moderate Rock Ballad

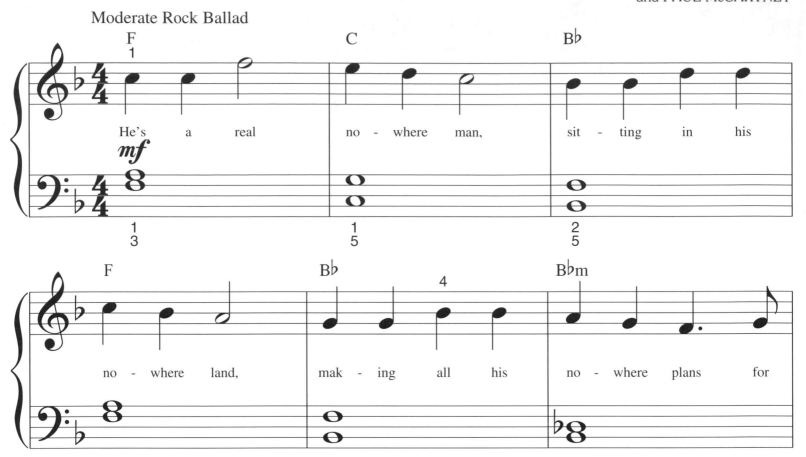

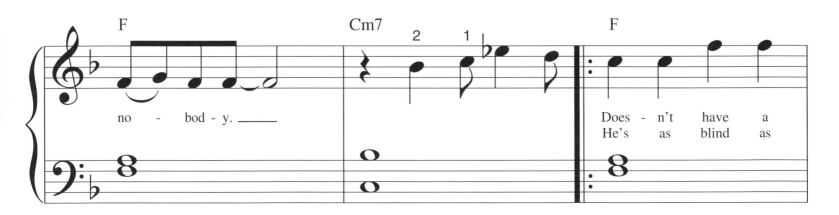

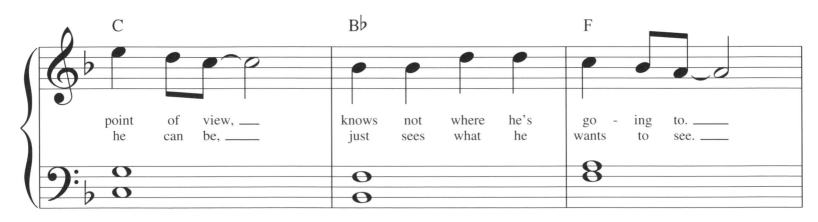

Is - n't he a bit like you and me? ____
No - where man, can you see me at all? ____

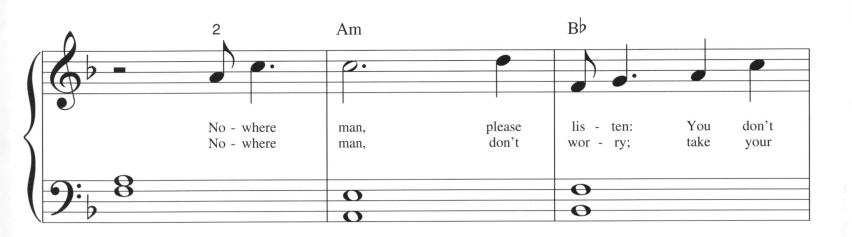

No - where man, please lis - ten: You don't
No - where man, don't wor - ry; You take your

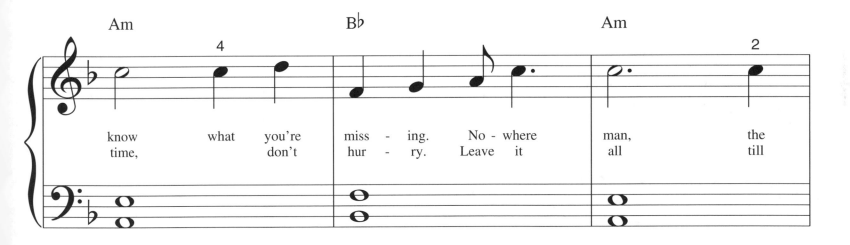

know what you're miss - ing. No - where man, the
time, don't hur - ry. Leave it all till

world ____ is at your com - mand.
some - bod - y else lends you a hand.

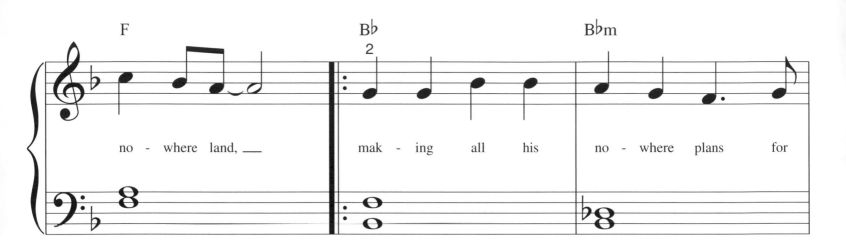

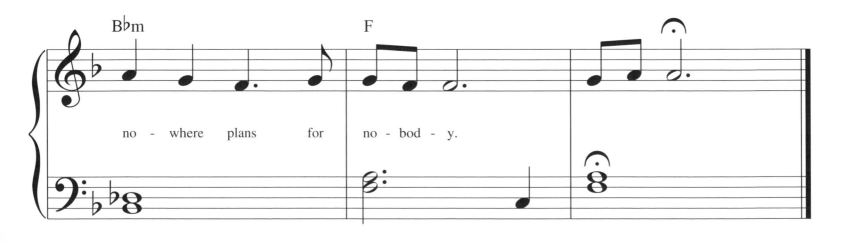

NORWEGIAN WOOD
(This Bird Has Flown)

Words and Music by JOHN LENNON
and PAUL McCARTNEY

Moderately flowing, in 1

I once had a girl, or should I say she once had me.

She showed me her room; isn't it good Norwegian wood? She

Dm

asked   me   to   stay   and   she   told   me   to   sit   an - y -
told   me   she   worked   in   the   morn - ing   and   start - ed   to

G   Dm

where. _____   So   I   looked   a -
laugh. _____   I   told   her   I

                                                                                Em7

round   and   I   no - ticed   there   was - n't   a   chair. _____
did - n't   and   crawled   off   to   sleep   in   the   bath. _____

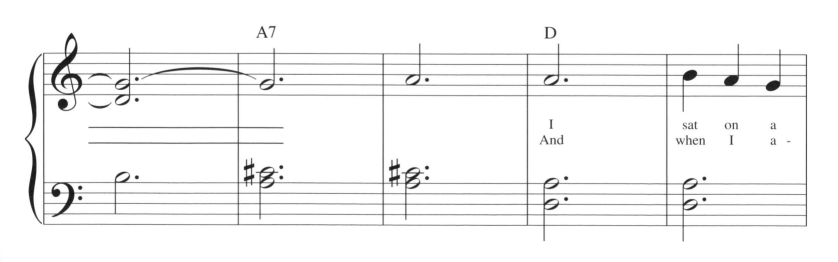

                    A7   D

                                        I   sat   on   a
                                        And   when   I   a -

SHE LOVES YOU

Words and Music by JOHN LENNON
and PAUL McCARTNEY

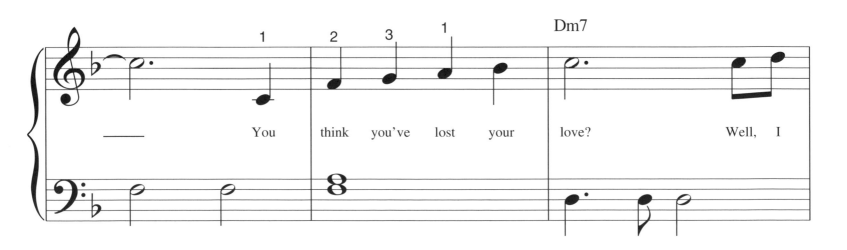

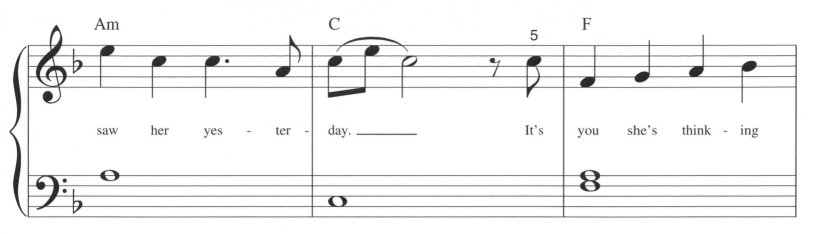

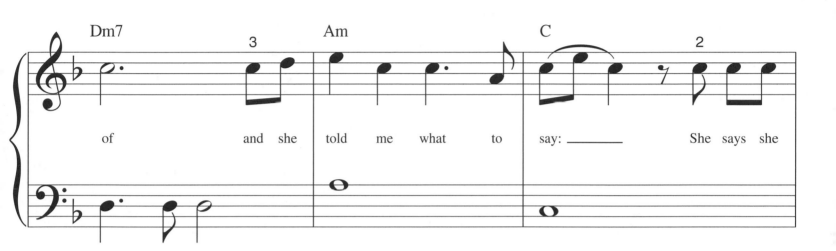

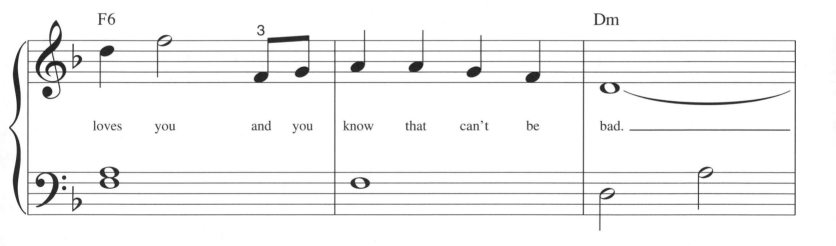

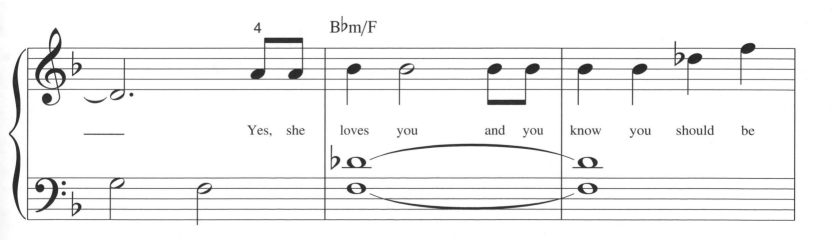

glad. _____

C

She said you hurt her
know it's up her to

F

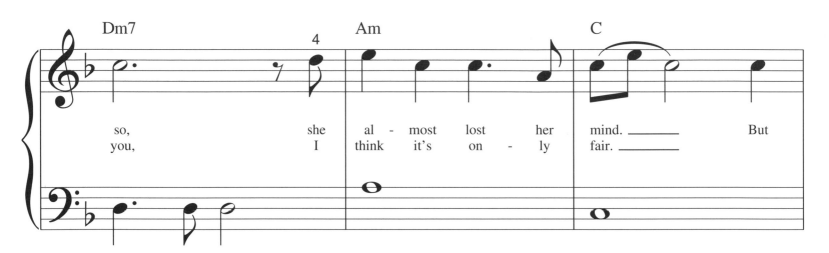

so,   she al - most lost her mind. _____ But
you,   I think it's on - ly fair. _____

Dm7   4   Am   C

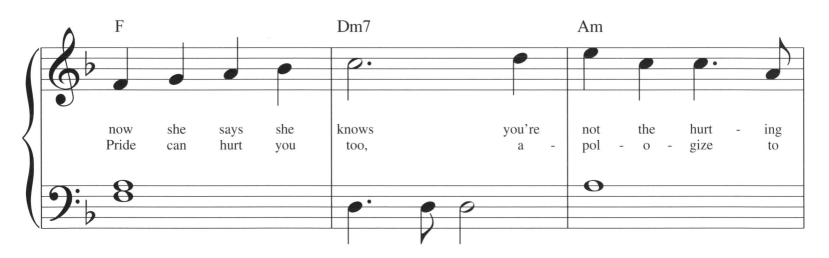

now she says she knows   you're   not the hurt - ing
Pride she can hurt you too,   a - pol - o - gize - ing to

F   Dm7   Am

kind. _____   She says she }   loves you   and you   know that can't be
her. _____   Be - cause she }

C   F6   3

bad. _____ Yes, she loves you and you

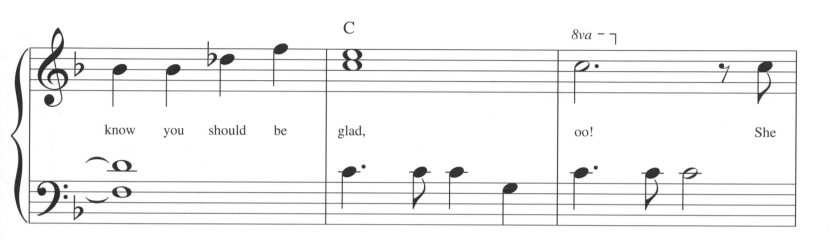

know you should be glad, oo! She

loves you, yeah, yeah, yeah, she loves you, yeah,

yeah, yeah. And with a love like that you know you should be

OB-LA-DI, OB-LA-DA

Words and Music by JOHN LENNON
and PAUL McCARTNEY

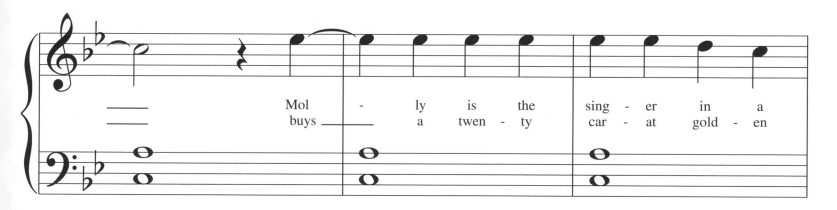

Des - mond has a bar - row in the mar - ket place, _
Des - mond takes a trol - ley to the jewel - er's store, _

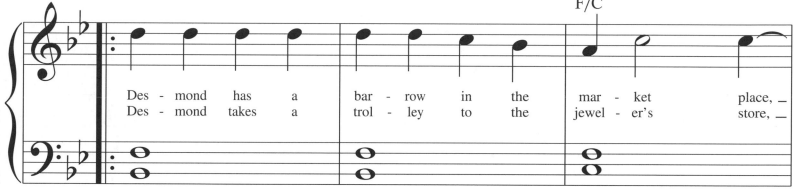

Mol - ly is the sing - er in a
buys _ a twen - ty car - at gold - en

band.
ring.

Des - mond says to
Takes _ it back to

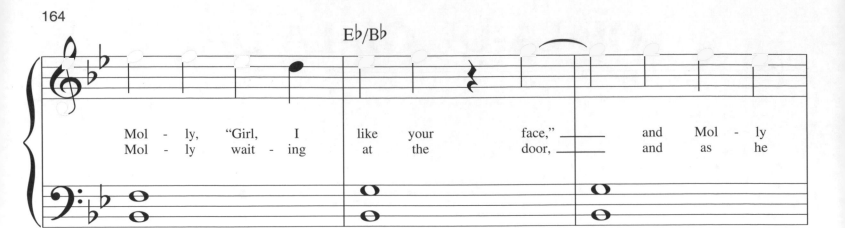

Mol - ly, "Girl, I like your face," and Mol - ly
Mol - ly wait - ing at the door, and as he

says this as she takes him by the hand: ___
gives it to her she be - gins to sing: ___

Ob - la - di, ___ Ob - la - da, ___ life goes on, ___

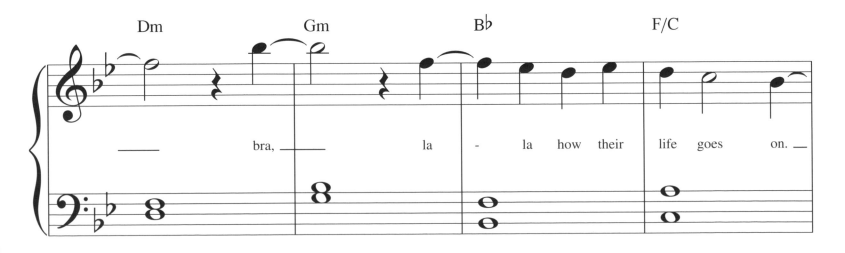

___ bra, ___ la - la how their life goes on.

Ob - la - di, _____ Ob - la - da, _____

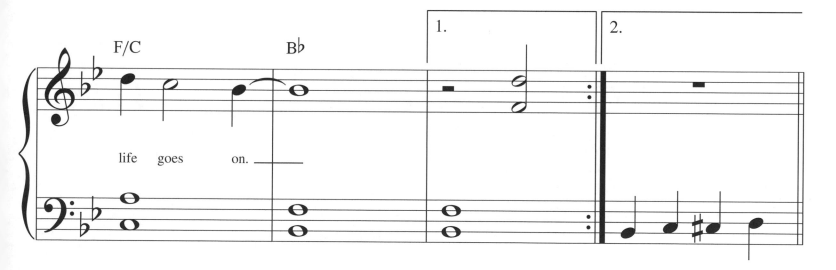

_____ life goes on, _____ bra, _____ la - la how their

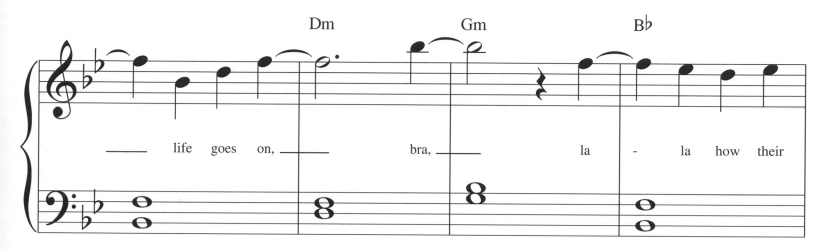

life goes on. _____

1. 2.

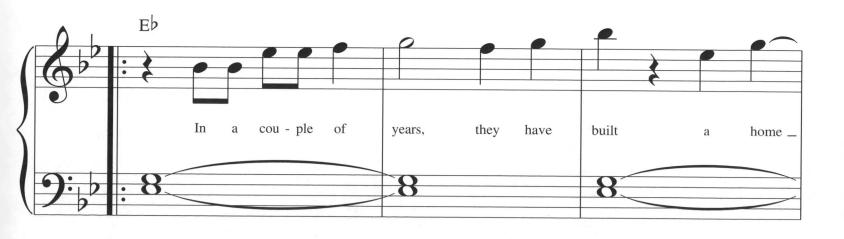

In a cou - ple of years, they have built a home ___

sweet home.

With a cou - ple of

kids run - ning in the yard ___ of

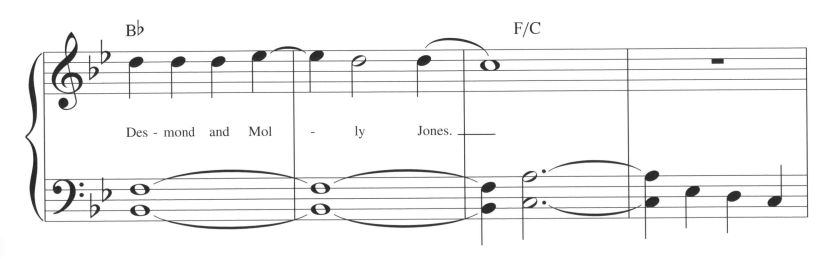

Des - mond and Mol - ly Jones. ___

Hap - py ev - er af - ter in the mar - ket place, ___
Hap - py ev - er af - ter in the mar - ket place, ___

___ Des - mond lets the chil - dren lend a
___ Mol - ly lets the chil - dren lend a

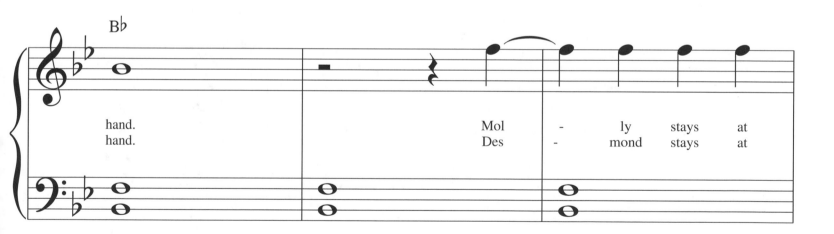

hand. Mol - ly stays at
hand. Des - mond stays at

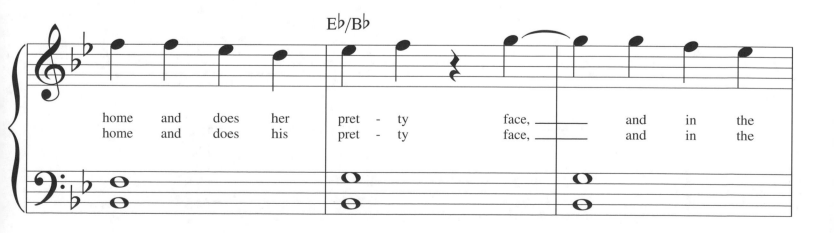

home and does her pret - ty face, ___ and in the
home and does his pret - ty face, ___ and in the

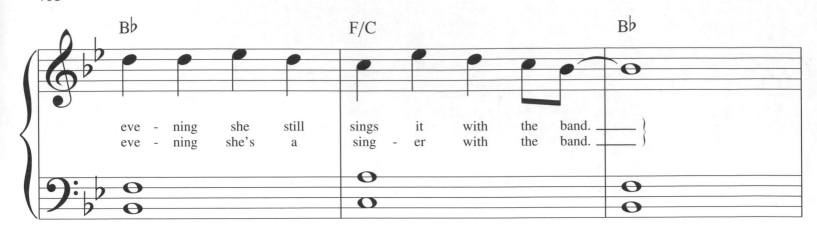

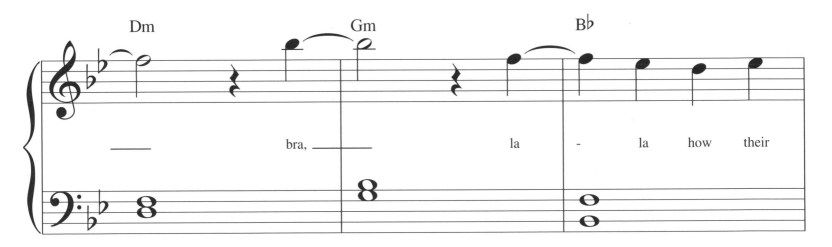

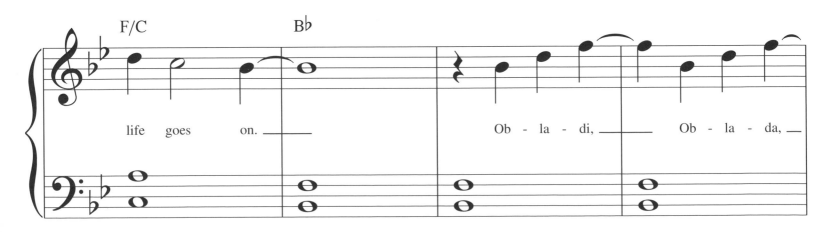

PAPERBACK WRITER

Words and Music by JOHN LENNON
and PAUL McCARTNEY

take a look? It's ____ based on a nov - el by a
week or two. I can make it ____ long - er if you

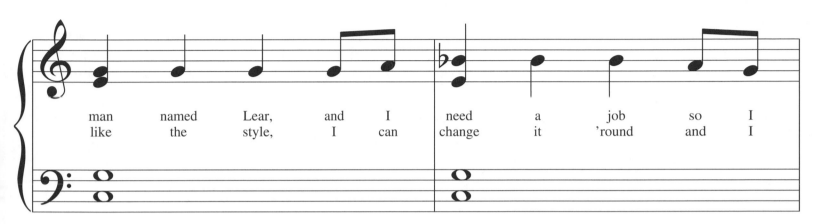

man named Lear, and I need a job so I
like the style, I can change it 'round and I

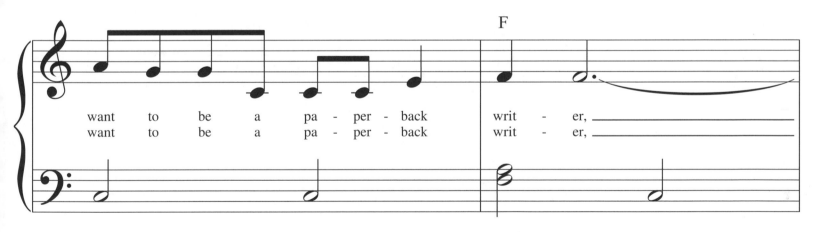

F

want to be a pa - per - back writ - er, ____
want to be a pa - per - back writ - er, ____

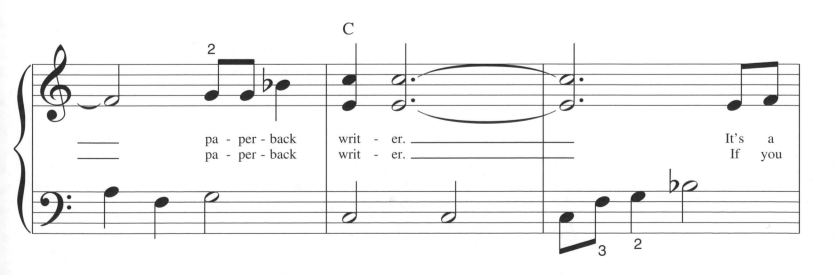

C

____ pa - per - back writ - er. ____
____ pa - per - back writ - er. ____ It's a
If you

dirt - y sto - ry of a dirt - y man, and his cling - ing wife does - n't
real - ly like it you can have the right, it could make a mil - lion for you

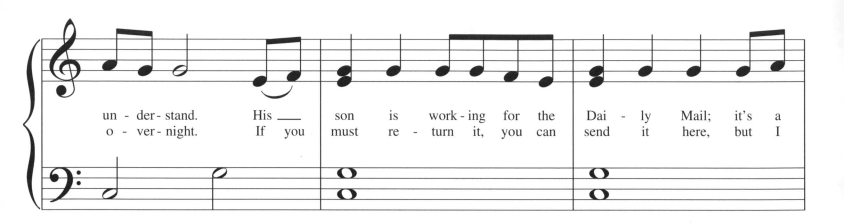

un - der - stand. His ___ son is work - ing for the Dai - ly Mail; it's a
o - ver - night. If you must re - turn it, you can send it here, but I

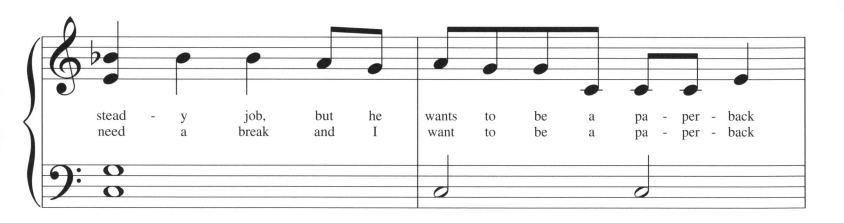

stead - y job, but he wants to be a pa - per - back
need a break and I want to be a pa - per - back

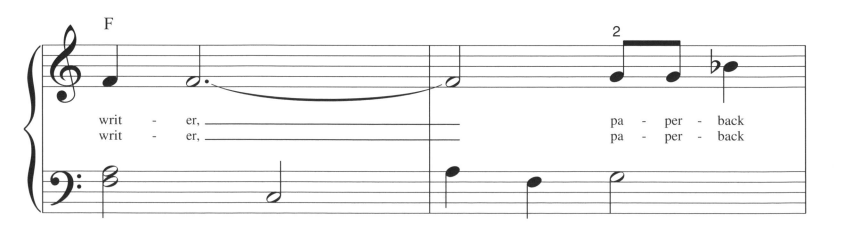

writ - er, _____ pa - per - back
writ - er, _____ pa - per - back

PENNY LANE

Words and Music by JOHN LENNON
and PAUL McCARTNEY

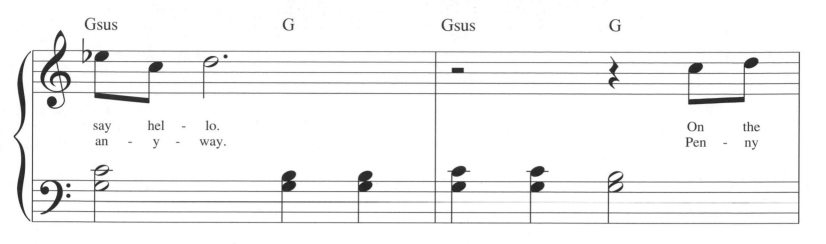

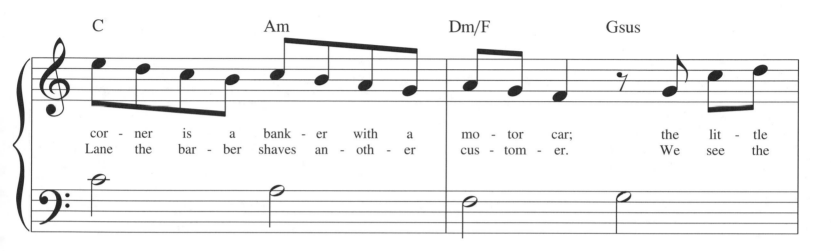

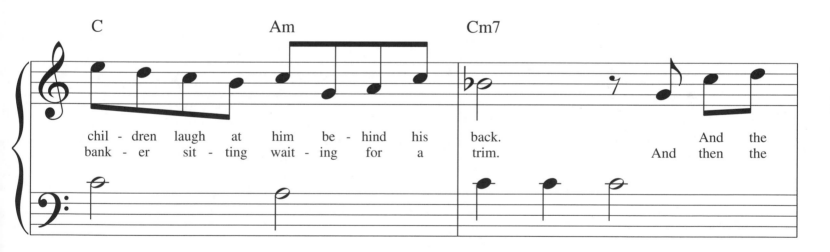

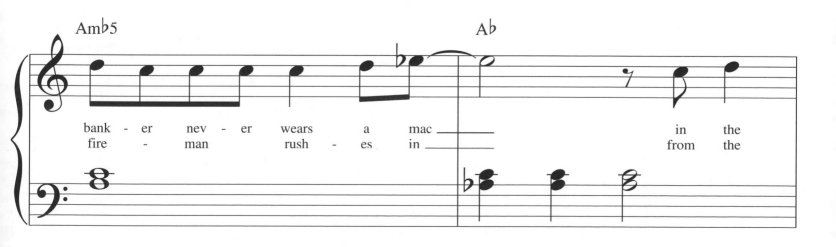

pour - ing rain, ver - y strange! Pen - ny Lane is in my ears __
pour - ing rain, ver - y strange! Pen - ny Lane is in my ears __

and in my eyes, __
and in my eyes, __

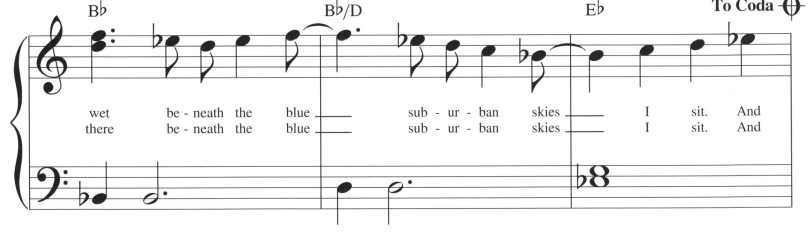

wet be - neath the blue __ sub - ur - ban skies __ I sit. And
there be - neath the blue __ sub - ur - ban skies __ I sit. And

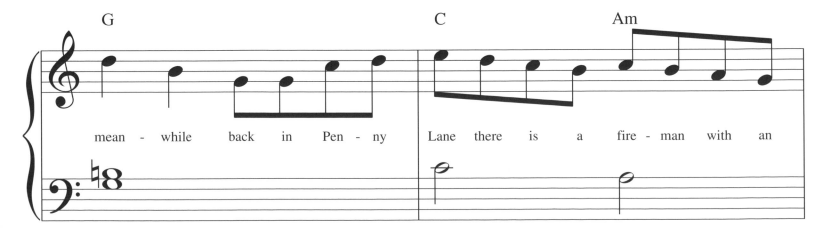

mean - while back in Pen - ny Lane there is a fire - man with an

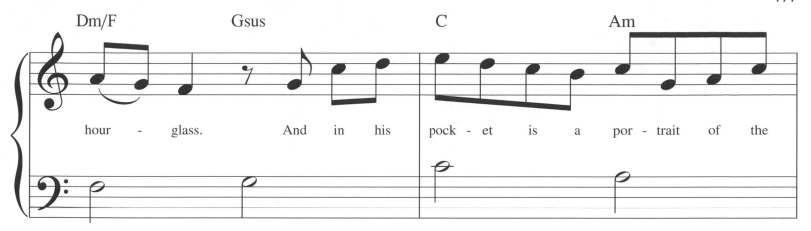

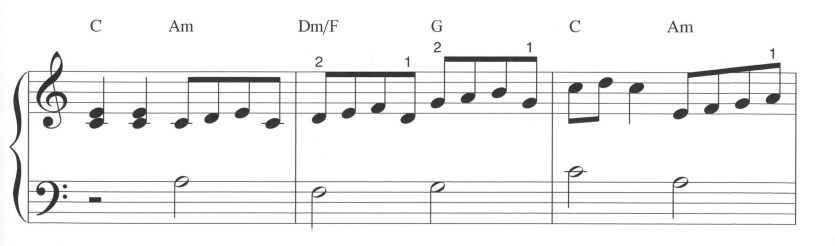

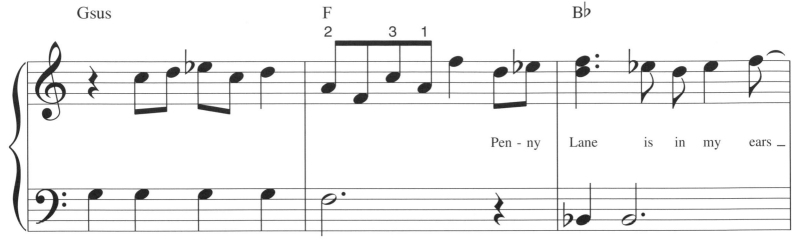

Pen - ny Lane is in my ears __

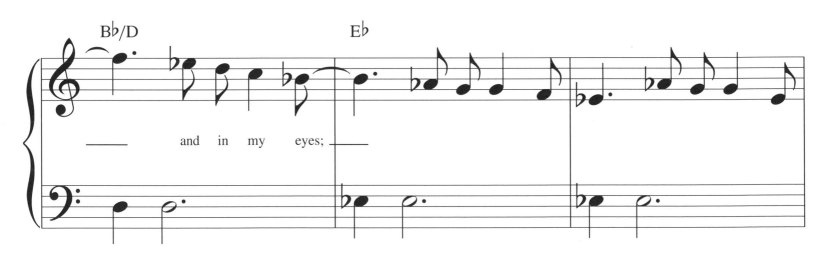

__ and in my eyes; __

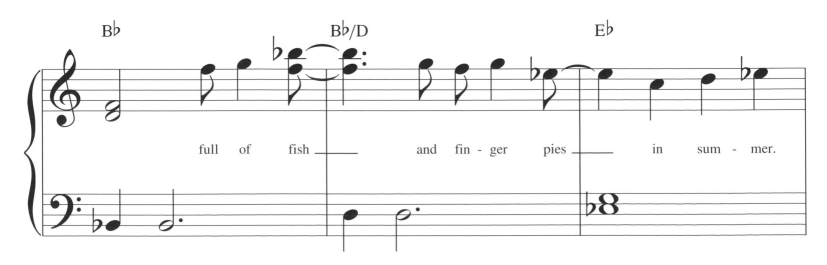

full of fish __ and fin - ger pies __ in sum - mer.

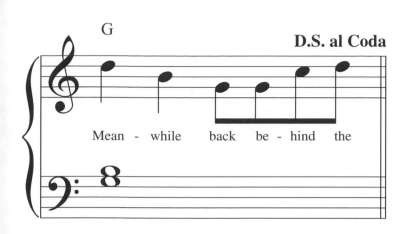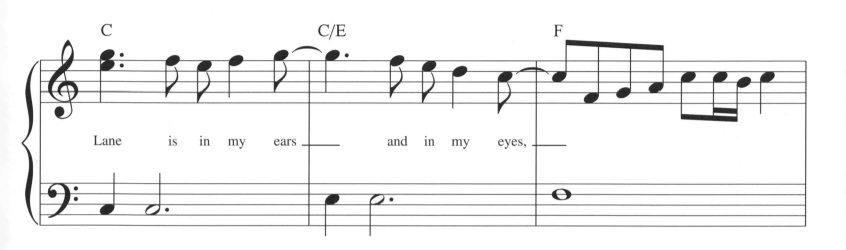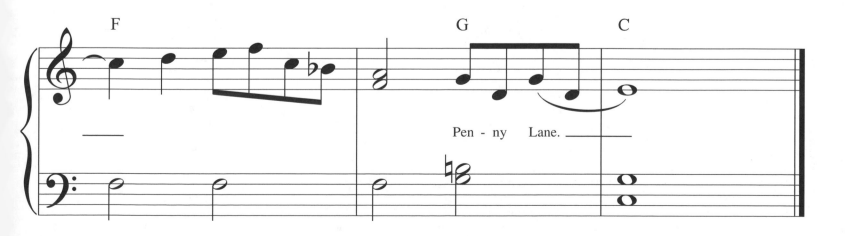

PLEASE PLEASE ME

Words and Music by JOHN LENNON
and PAUL McCARTNEY

Moderately, with a beat

Last night I said these words to
You don't I need to show to the

my _____ girl,
way, _____ love,

I know you nev - er e - ven
why do I al - ways have to

try, _____ girl. _____
say, _____ love. _____

Come

on, (come on) _____ come on, (come on) _____ come

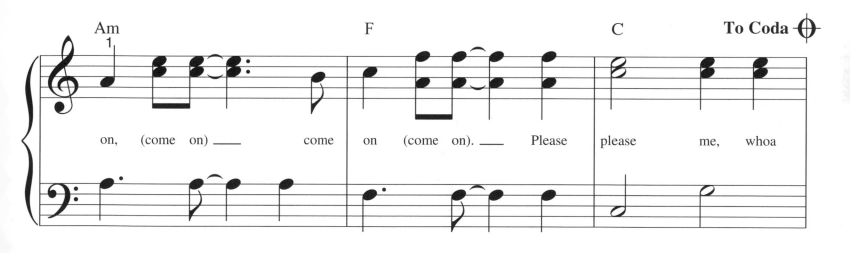

on, (come on) _____ come on (come on). _____ Please please me, whoa

To Coda ⊕

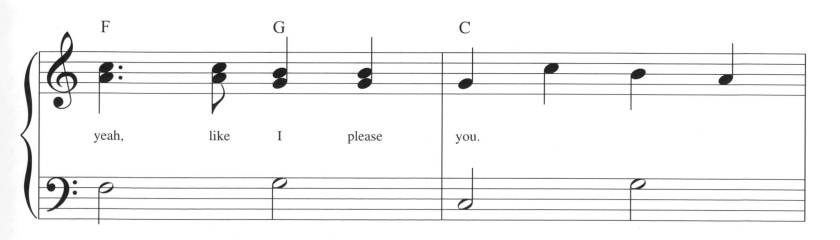

yeah, like I please you.

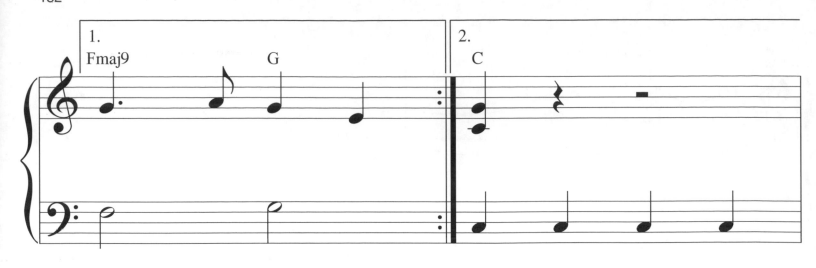

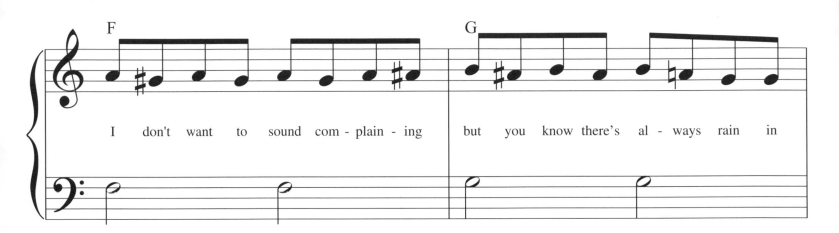

I don't want to sound com - plain - ing but you know there's al - ways rain in

my _____ heart (in _____ my heart).

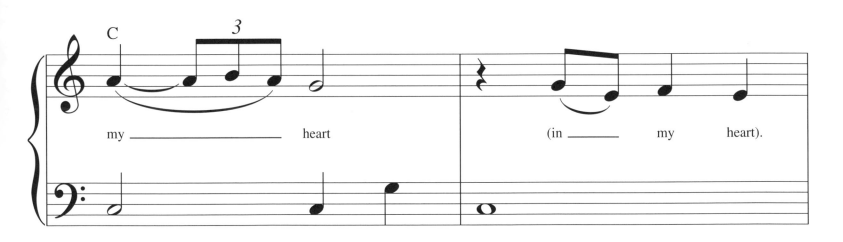

I do all the pleas - ing with you, it's so hard to rea - son with

D.S. al Coda
(Verse 1)

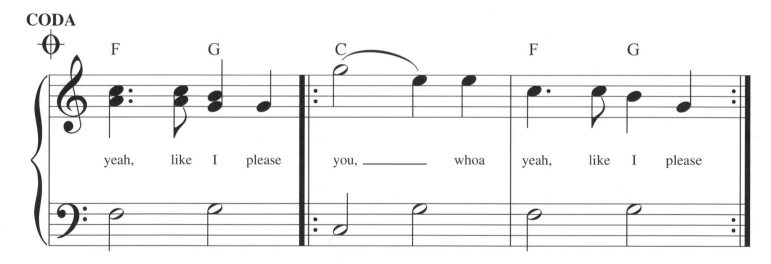

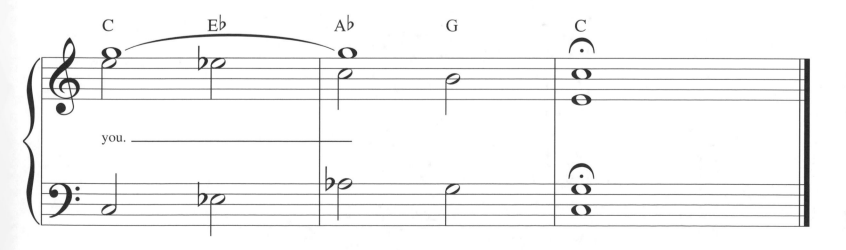

REVOLUTION

Words and Music by JOHN LENNON
and PAUL McCARTNEY

say you want a rev-o-lu-tion, _____ well _____
say you got a real so-lu-tion, _____ well _____
say you'll change the con-sti-tu-tion, _____ well _____

_____ you know, _____ we all want to change the
_____ you know, _____ we'd all love to see the
_____ you know, _____ we all want to change your

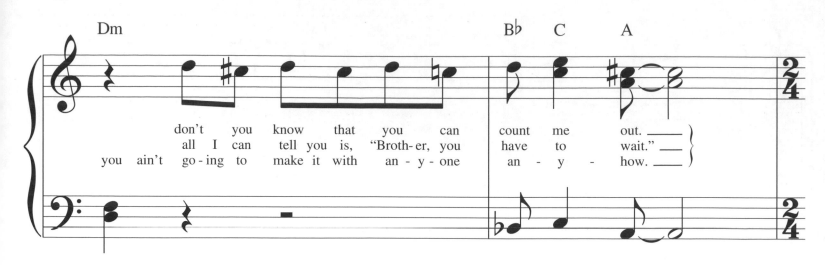

don't you know that you can count me out. ___
all I can tell you is, "Broth- er, you have to wait." ___
you ain't go - ing to make it with an - y - one an - y - how. ___

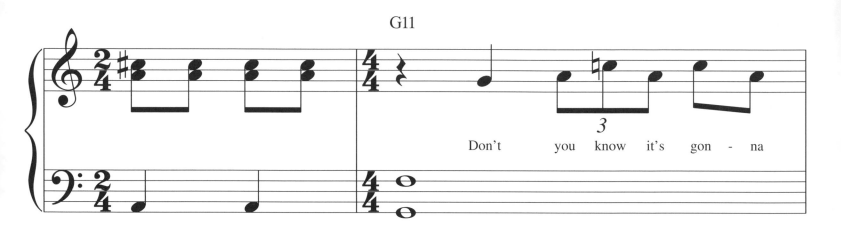

Don't you know it's gon - na

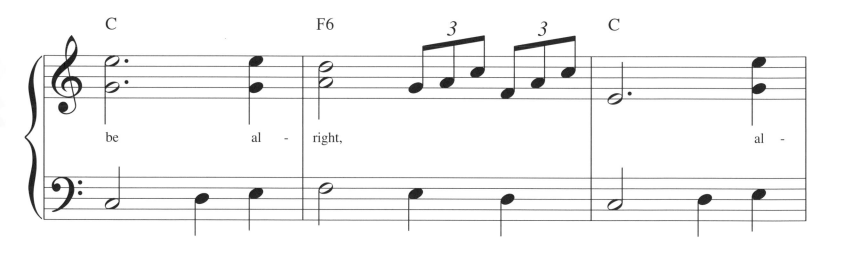

be al - right, al -

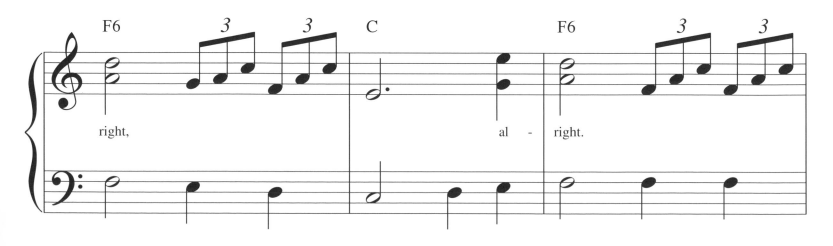

right, al - right.

RUN FOR YOUR LIFE

Words and Music by JOHN LENNON
and PAUL McCARTNEY

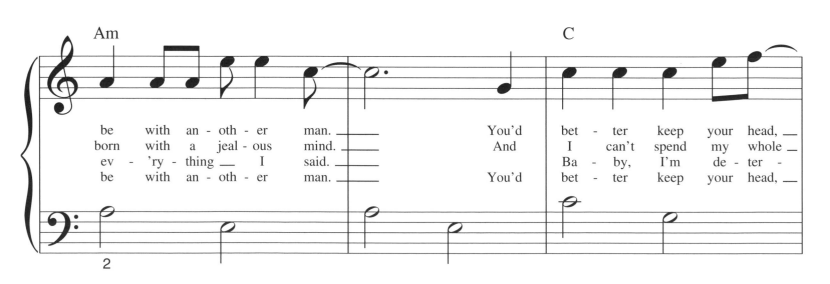

Well, you
I'd

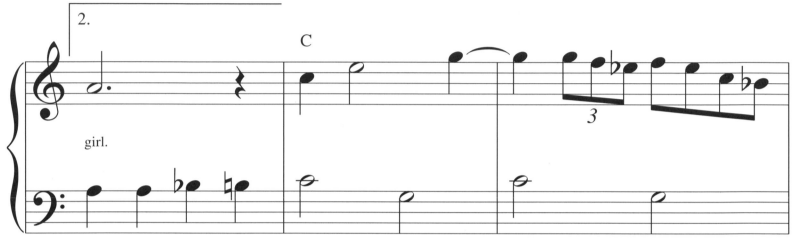

2.

girl.

C

3

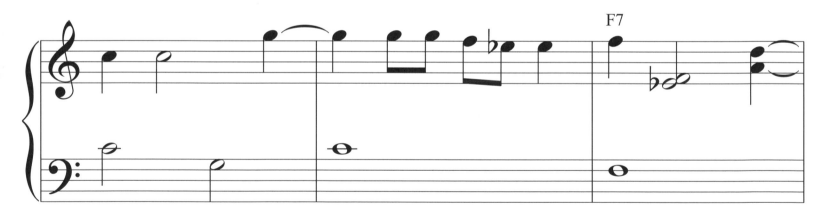

F7

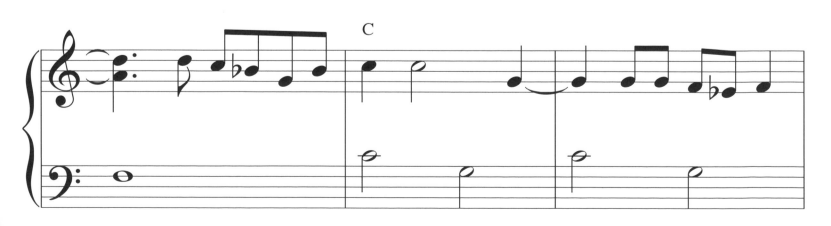

C

191

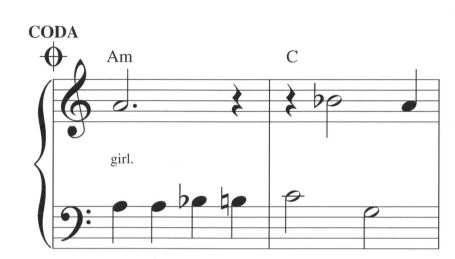

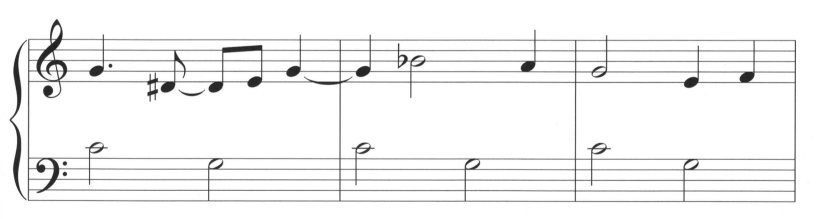

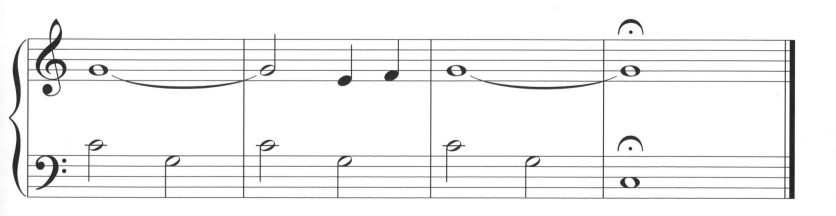

SGT. PEPPER'S LONELY HEARTS CLUB BAND

Words and Music by JOHN LENNON
and PAUL McCARTNEY

Moderately slow, with a strong beat

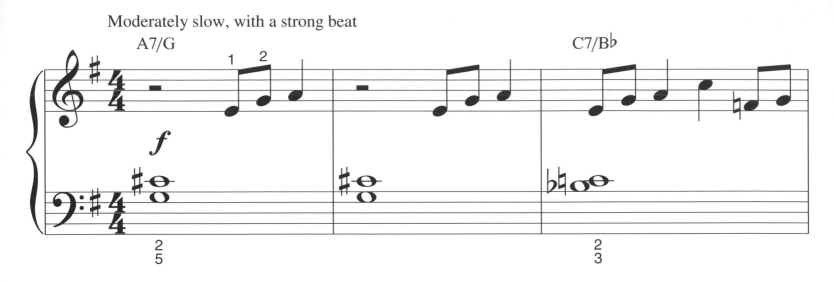

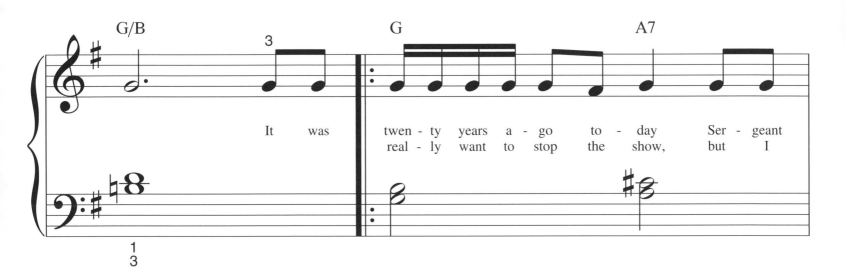

It was twen-ty years a-go to-day Ser-geant
real-ly want to stop the show, but I

Pep-per taught the band to play. They've been
thought you might like to know that the

go-ing in and out of style, but they're
sing-er's going to sing a song, and he

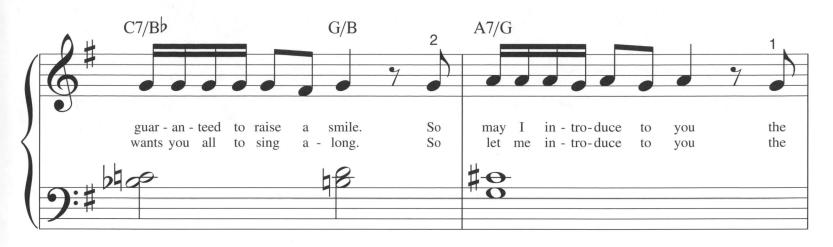

guar - an - teed to raise a smile. So
wants you all to sing a - long. So

may I in - tro-duce to you the
let me in - tro-duce to you the

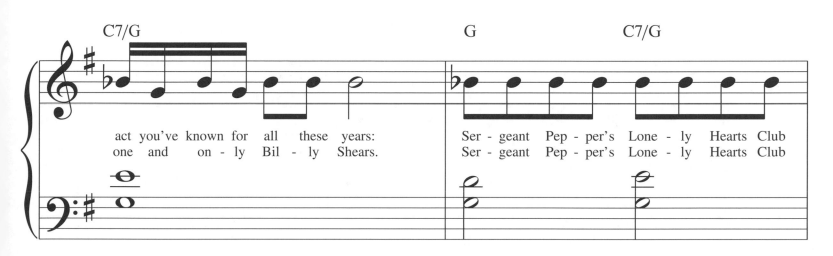

act you've known for all these years:
one and on - ly Bil - ly Shears.

Ser - geant Pep - per's Lone - ly Hearts Club
Ser - geant Pep - per's Lone - ly Hearts Club

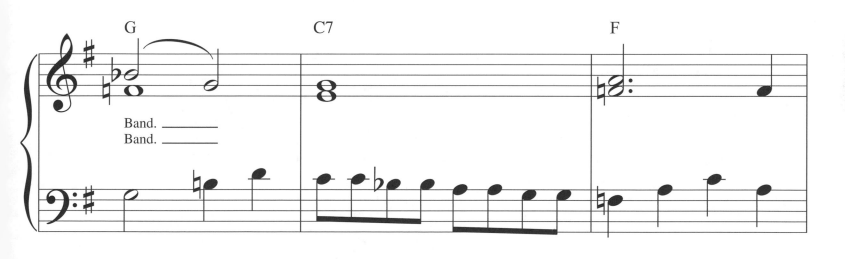

Band. _____
Band. _____

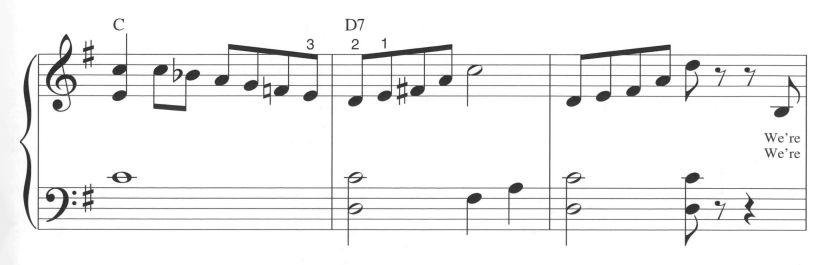

We're
We're

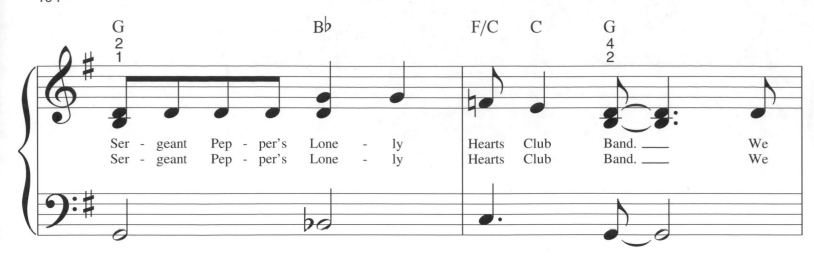

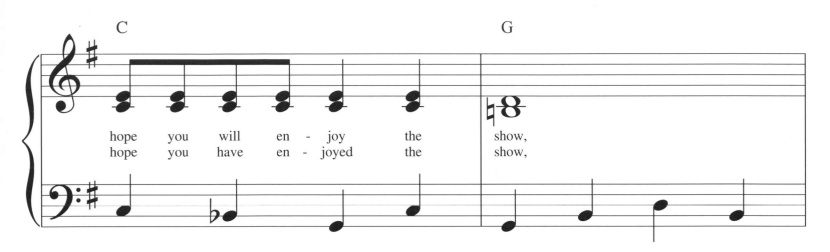

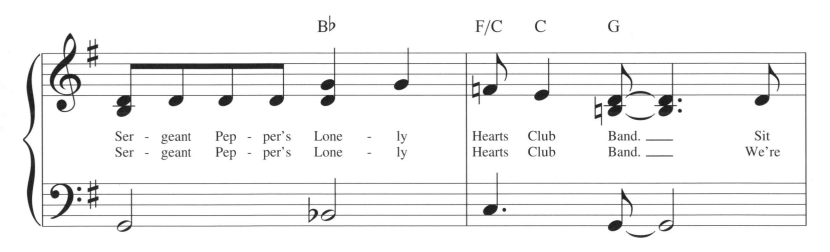

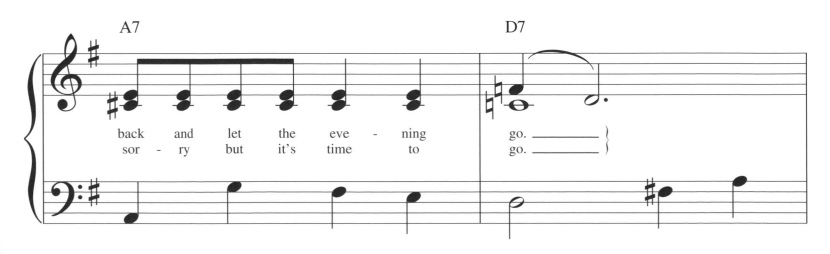

SOMETHING

Words and Music by
GEORGE HARRISON

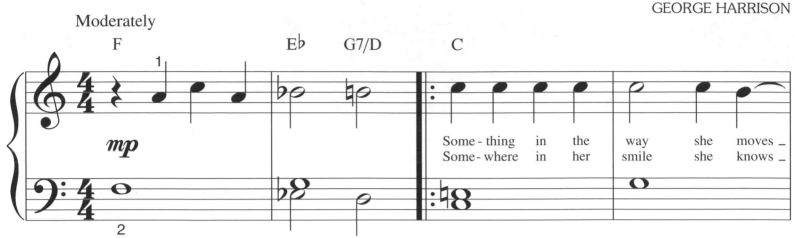

Moderately

Some - thing in the way she moves __
Some - where in her smile she knows __

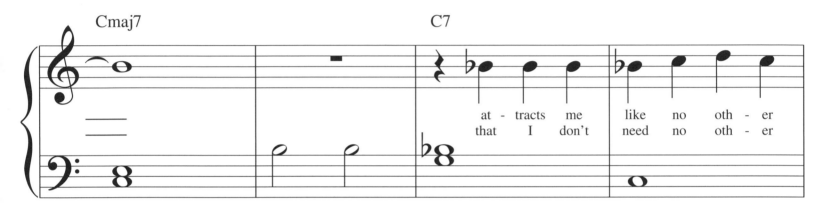

at - tracts me like no oth - er
that I don't need no oth - er

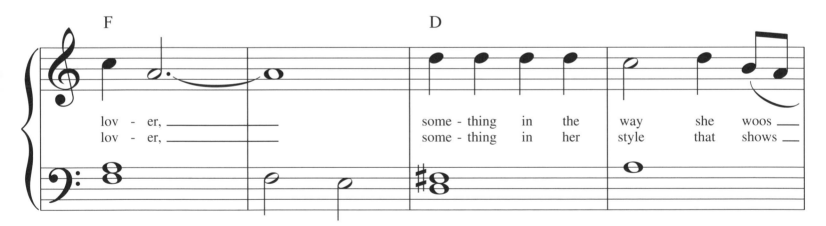

lov - er, __
lov - er, __
some - thing in the way she woos __
some - thing in her way style that shows __

me.
me.
I don't want to leave __ her now,

You stick a - round now, it may show;   I don't

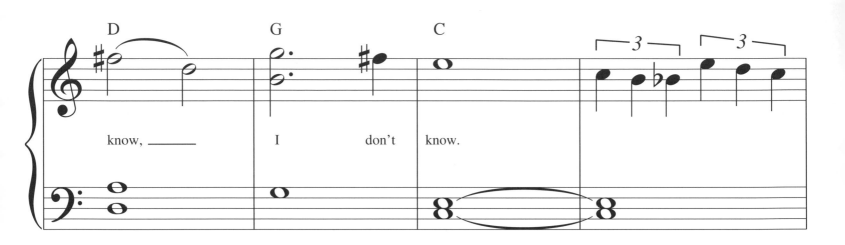

know,   I don't know.

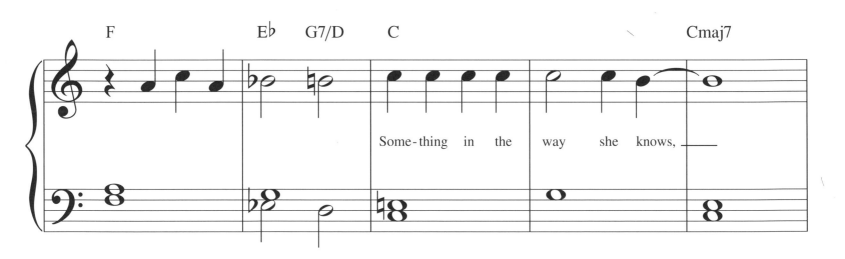

Some-thing in the way she knows,

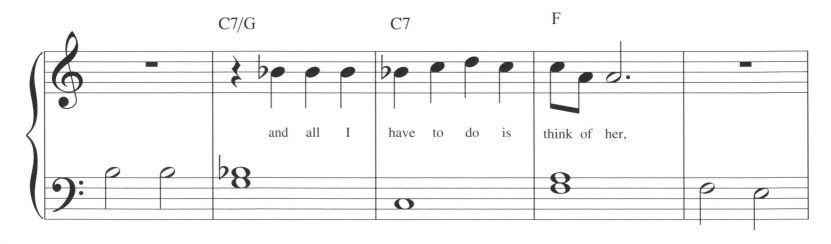

and all I have to do is think of her,

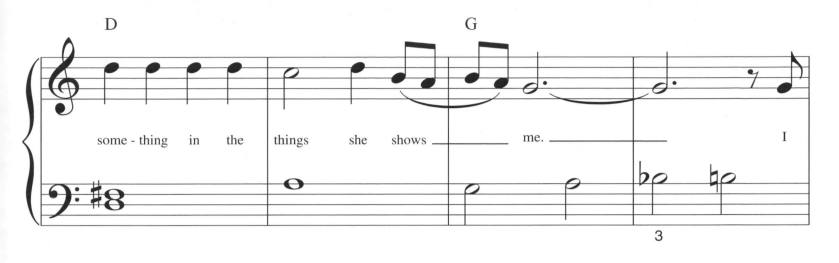

some-thing in the things she shows ____ me. ____ I

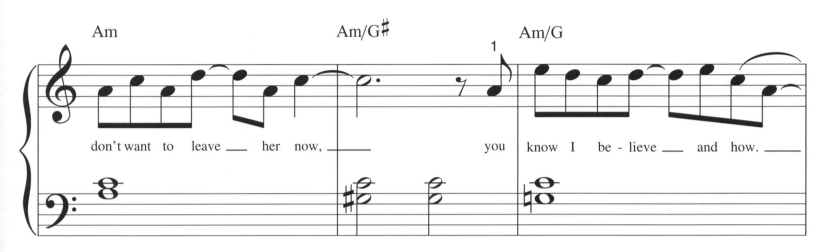

don't want to leave ____ her now, ____ you know I be-lieve ____ and how. ____

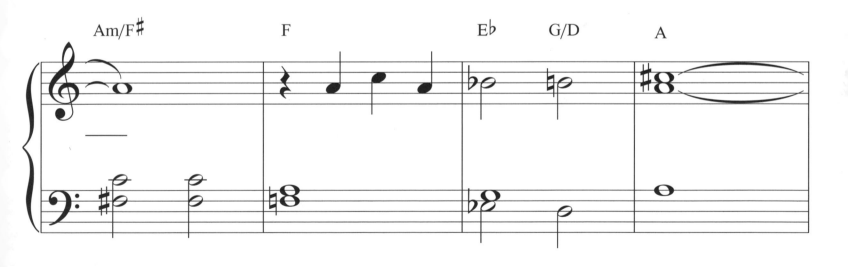

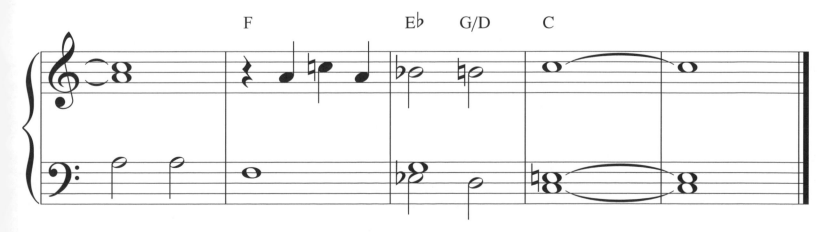

STRAWBERRY FIELDS FOREVER

Words and Music by JOHN LENNON
and PAUL McCARTNEY

Slowly, but not dragging

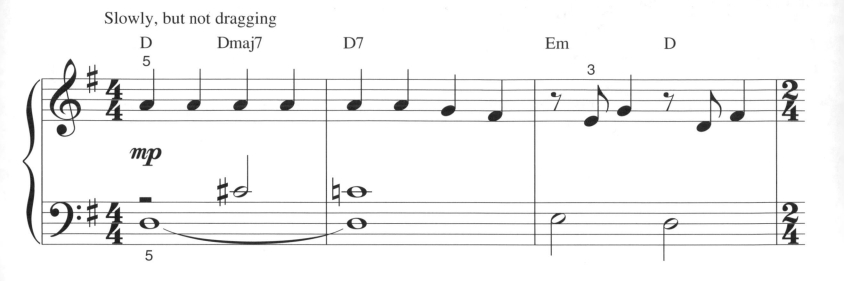

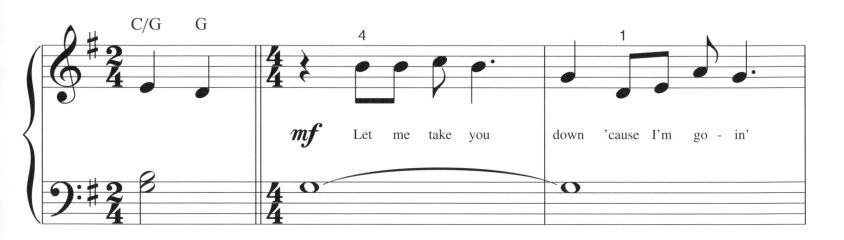

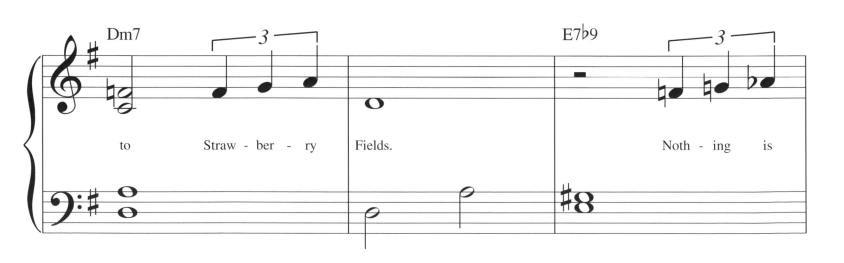

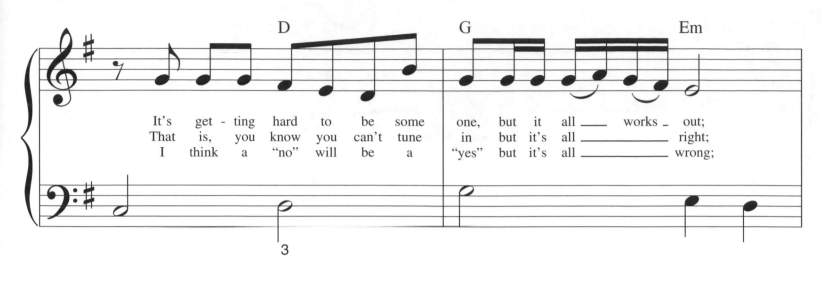

It's get-ting hard to be some one, but it all ___ works __ out;
That is, you know you can't tune in but it's all _____ right;
I think a "no" will be a "yes" but it's all _____ wrong;

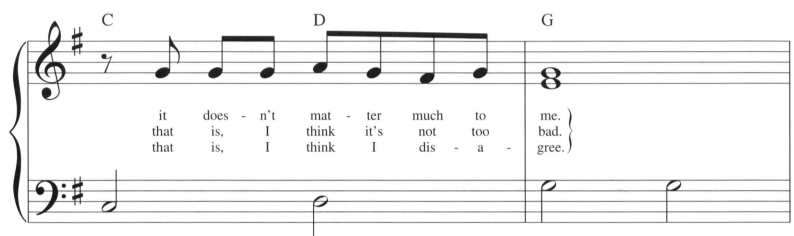

it does — n't mat — ter much to me.
that is, I think it's not too bad.
that is, I think I dis — a — gree.

Let me take you down 'cause I'm go — in' to Straw — ber — ry

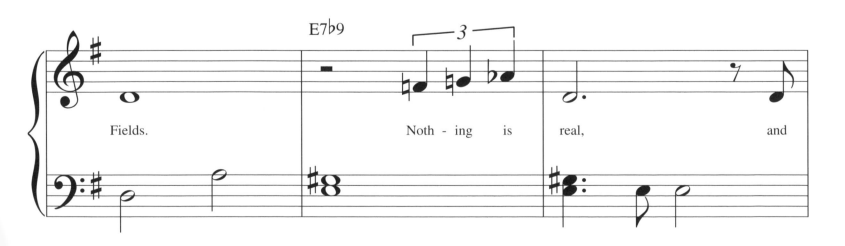

Fields. Noth — ing is real, and

TELL ME WHY

Words and Music by JOHN LENNON
and PAUL McCARTNEY

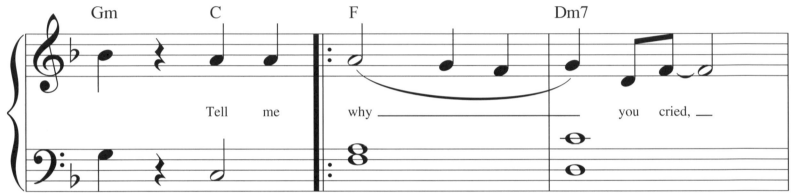

Tell me why _____ you cried, ___

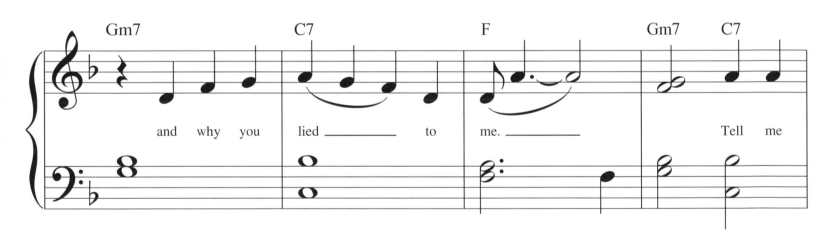

and why you lied _____ to me. _____ Tell me

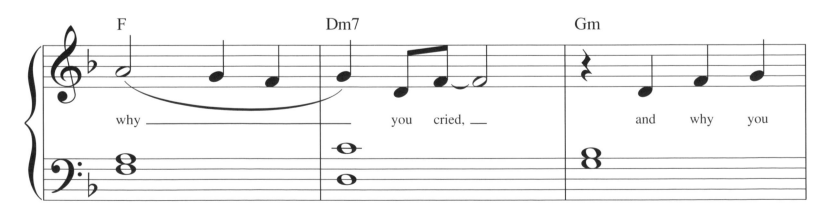

why _____ you cried, ___ and why you

lied _____ to ___ me.

Well, I gave _
If it's some -

___ you ev-'ry-thing I
- thing that I've said or

had, ___ but you
done, ___ tell me

left me sit-ting on my own. _
what, and I'll a-pol-o-gize. _

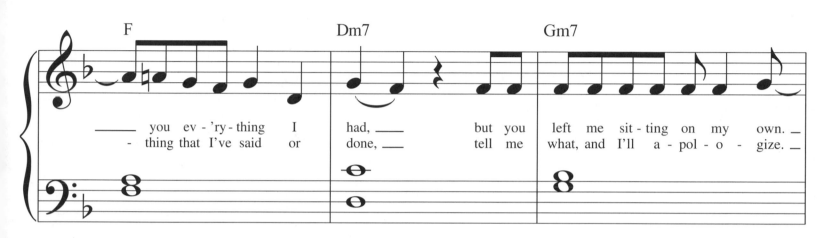

___
___

Did you have ___ to treat me oh, so bad? ___
If you don't, ___ I real-ly can't go on ___

All I
hold-ing

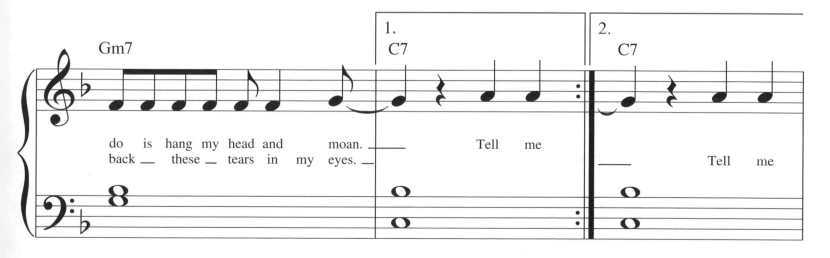

do is hang my head and moan. ___
back ___ these ___ tears in my eyes. ___

1.
Tell me

2.
___ Tell me

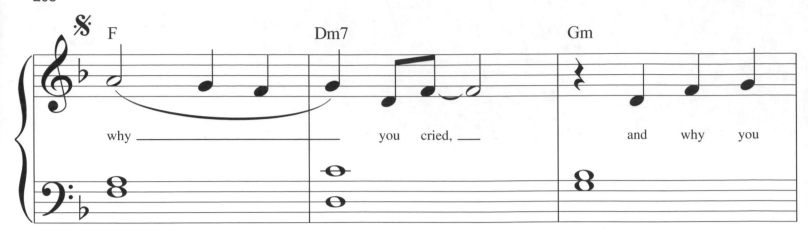

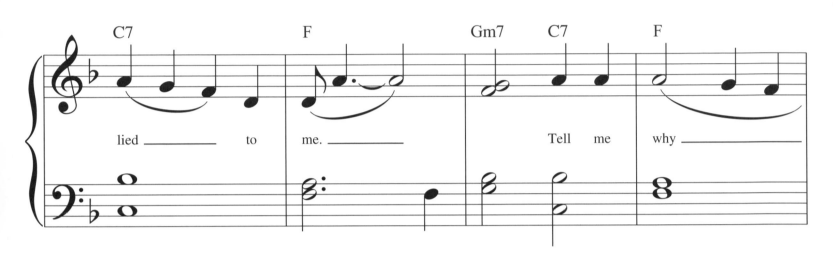

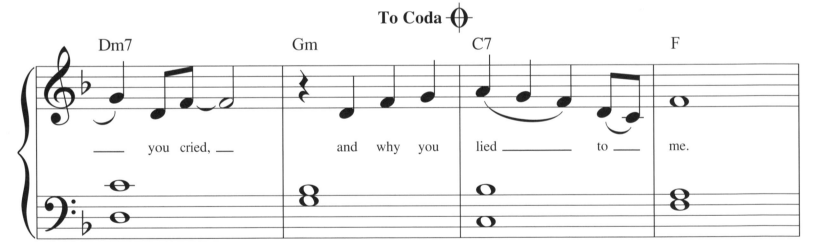

209

on - ly lis - ten to my pleas. ___ Is there an - y - thing I can

do, _____ 'cause I real - ly can't stand ___ it, I'm so ___ in love with ___

D.S. al Coda

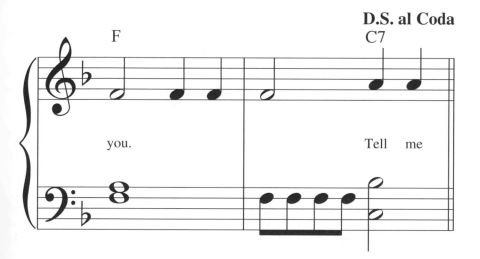

you. Tell me

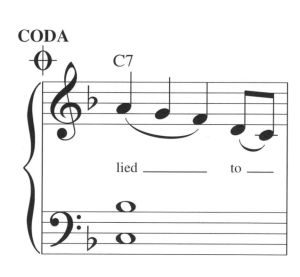

lied _____ to ___

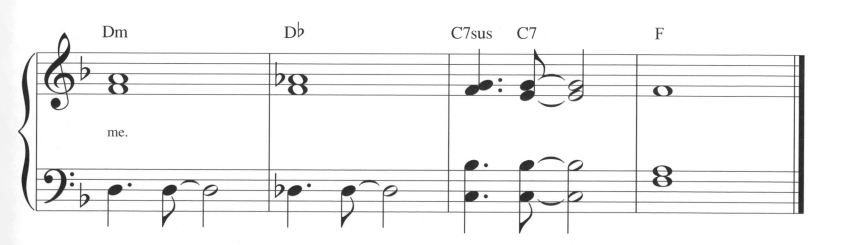

me.

TICKET TO RIDE

Words and Music by JOHN LENNON
and PAUL McCARTNEY

Moderate Rock

(1.) I think I'm gon-na be sad, ___ I think it's to-day, ___
(2.,3.) said that liv-ing with me ___ is bring-in' her down, ___

yeah! The girl that's driv-ing me mad ___
yeah! For she would nev-er be free ___

is go-ing a-way. ___
when I was a-round. ___

She's got a tick-et to ride, ___ she's got a tick-et to ri-

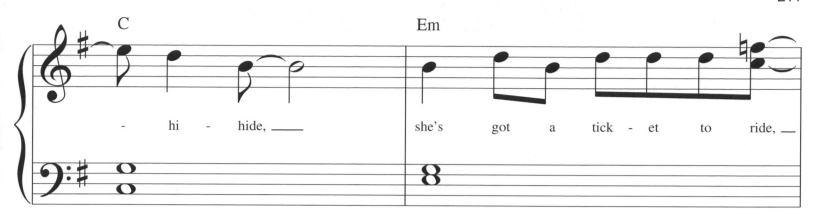

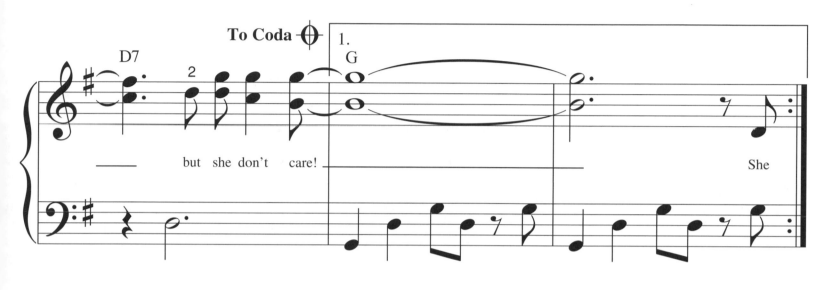

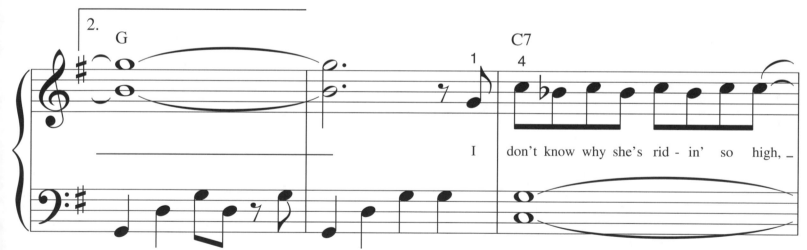

WE CAN WORK IT OUT

Words and Music by JOHN LENNON
and PAUL McCARTNEY

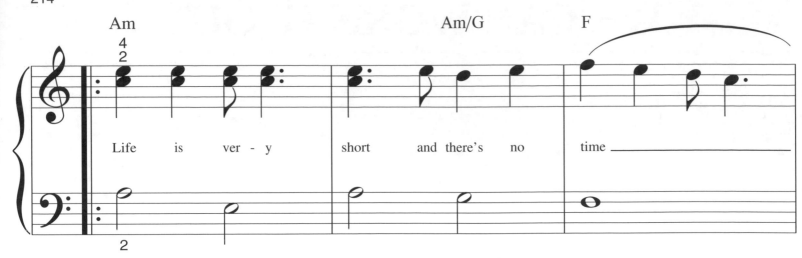

Life is ver - y short and there's no time _____

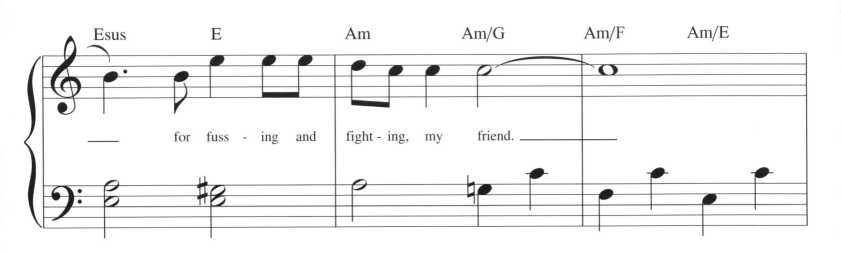

_____ for fuss - ing and fight - ing, my friend. _____

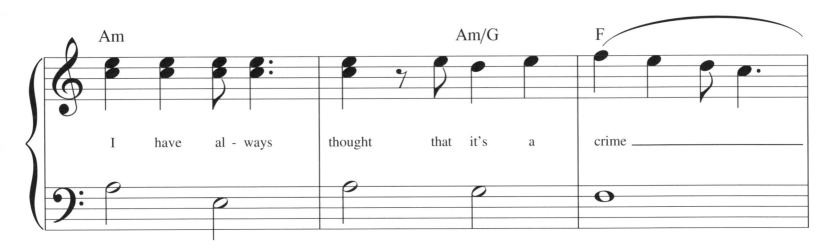

I have al - ways thought that it's a crime _____

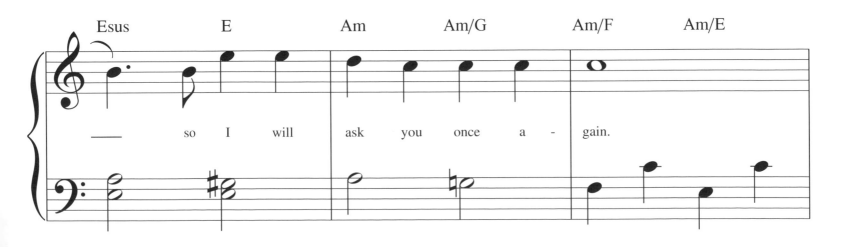

_____ so I will ask you once a - gain.

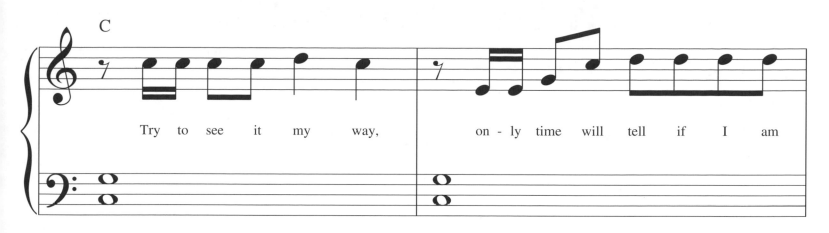

Try to see it my way, on - ly time will tell if I am

right or I am wrong. While you see it your way

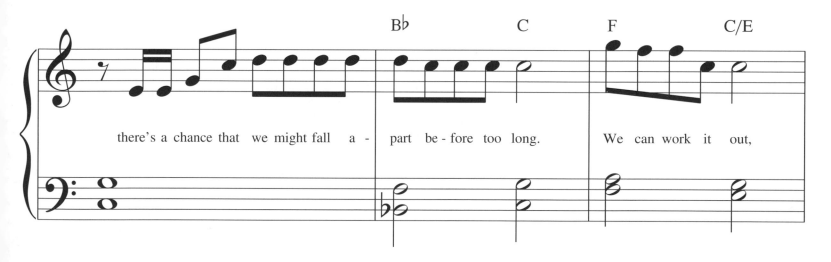

there's a chance that we might fall a - part be - fore too long. We can work it out,

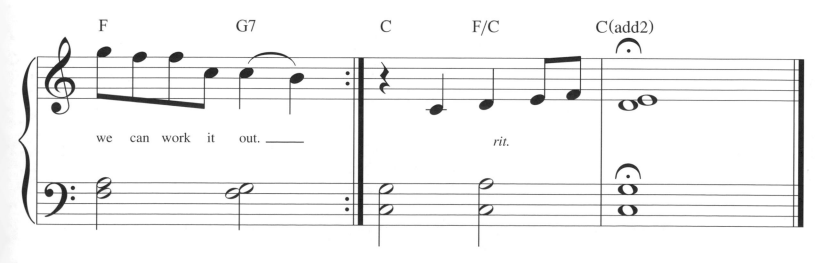

we can work it out. ___ *rit.*

TWIST AND SHOUT

Words and Music by BERT RUSSELL
and PHIL MEDLEY

WHEN I'M SIXTY-FOUR

Words and Music by JOHN LENNON
and PAUL McCARTNEY

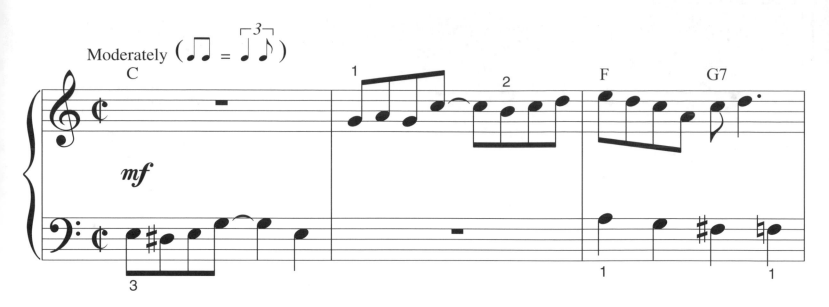

When I get old - er,   los - ing my hair, ___
I could be hand - y   mend - ing a fuse ___
Send me a post - card,   drop me a line ___

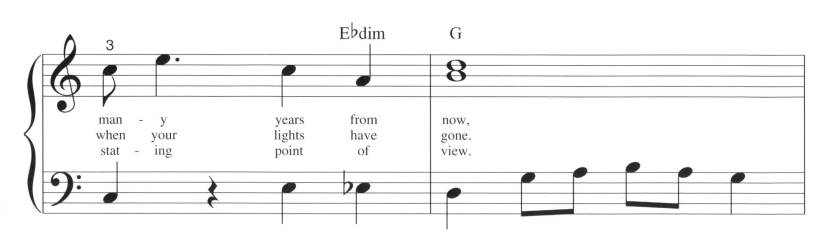

man - y   years   from   now,
when your   lights   have   gone.
stat - ing   point   of   view.

219

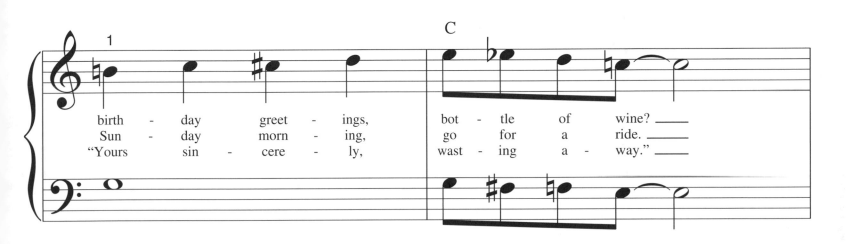

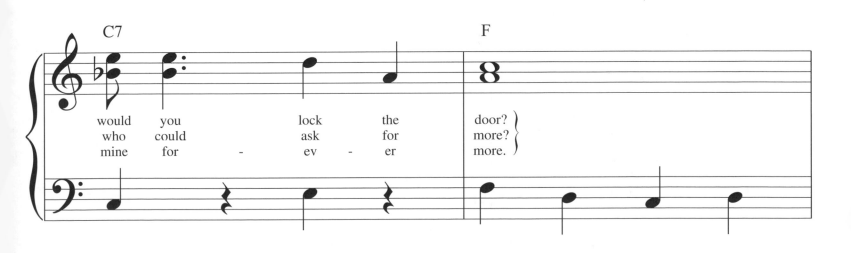

F#dim   C/G   A/C#

Will you still need ____ me, will you still feed ____ me,

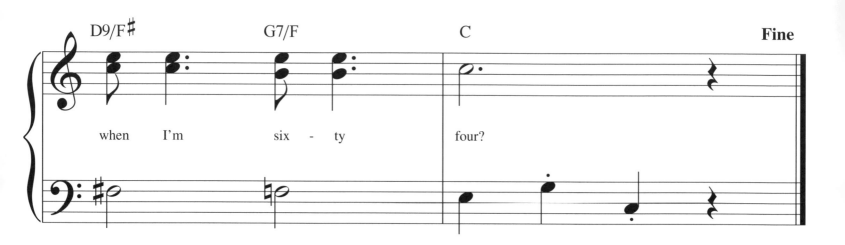

D9/F#   G7/F   C   **Fine**

when I'm six - ty four?

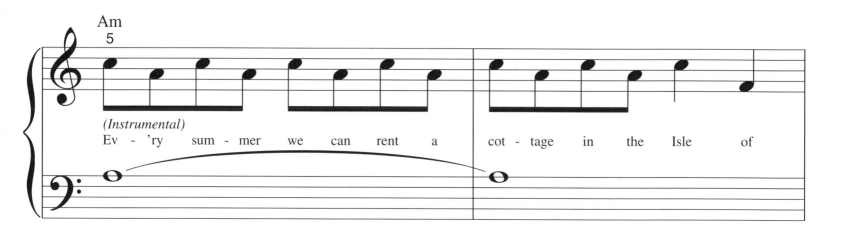

Am
5

(Instrumental)
Ev - 'ry sum - mer we can rent a cot - tage in the Isle of

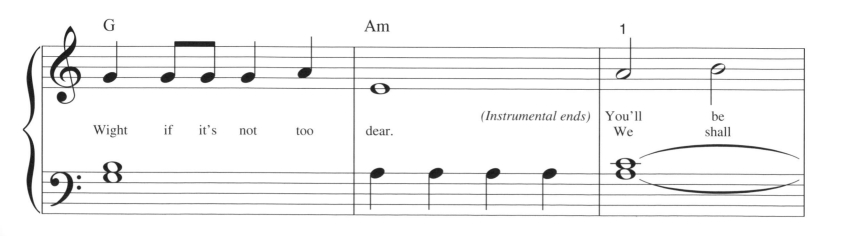

G   Am   1

Wight if it's not too dear.   *(Instrumental ends)* You'll be
We shall

WITH A LITTLE HELP FROM MY FRIENDS

Words and Music by JOHN LENNON
and PAUL McCARTNEY

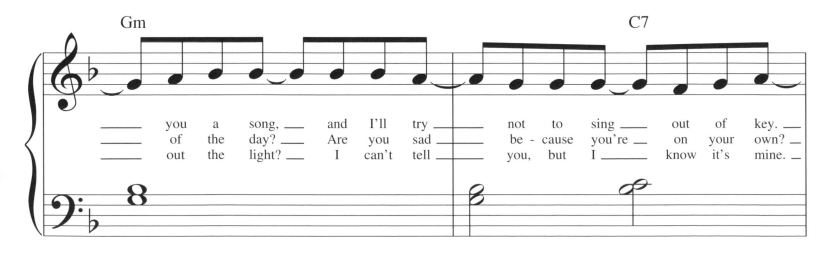

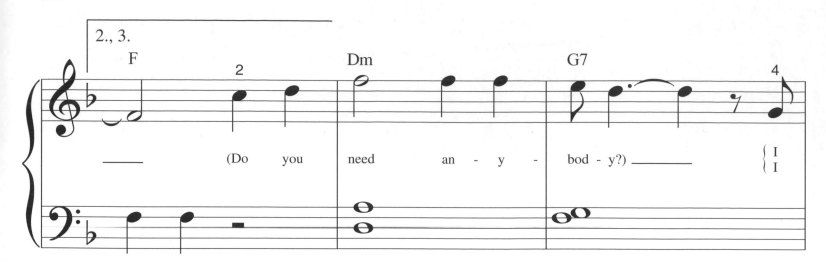

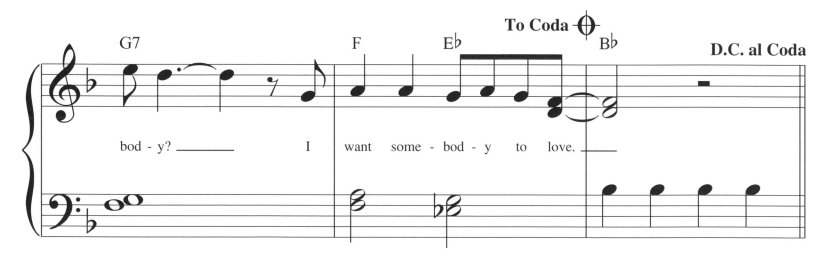

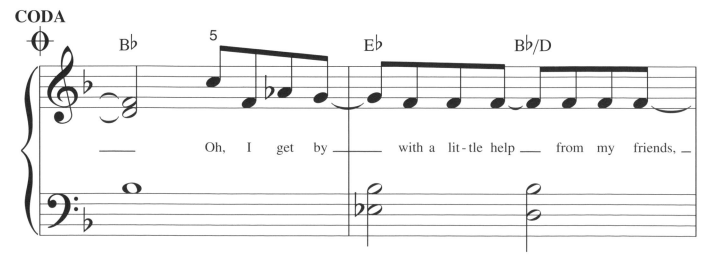

YELLOW SUBMARINE

Words and Music by JOHN LENNON
and PAUL McCARTNEY

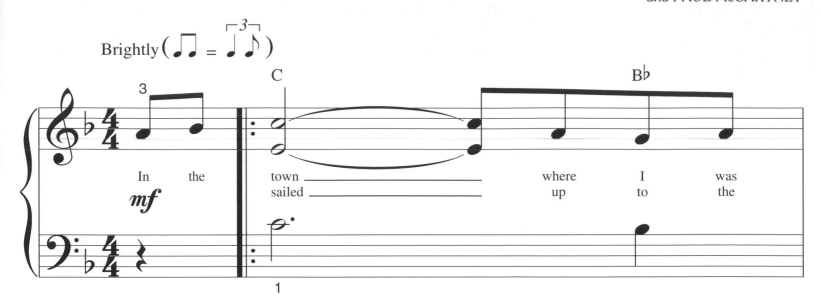

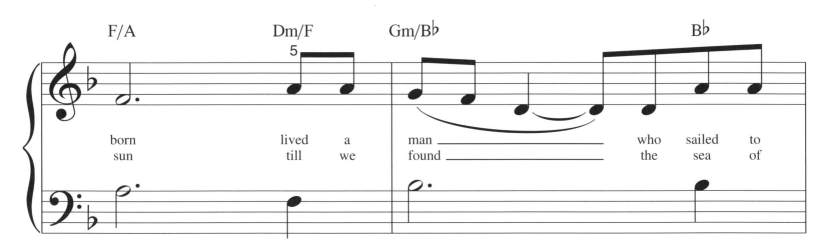

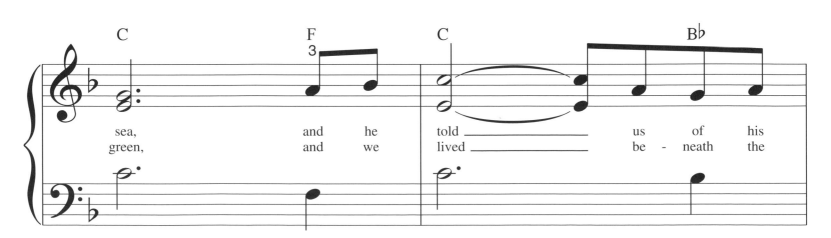

228

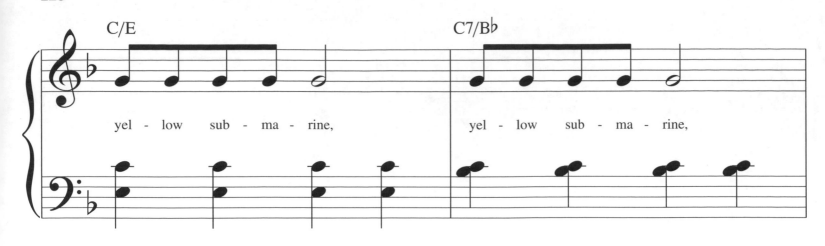

C/E yel - low sub - ma - rine,

C7/B♭ yel - low sub - ma - rine,

F/A yel - low sub - ma - rine.

{ And our
As we

C friends _____ are all on
live _____ a life of

B♭

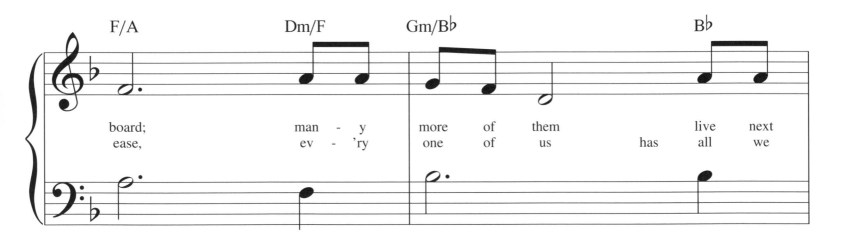

F/A board;
ease,

Dm/F man - y
ev - 'ry

Gm/B♭ more of them
one of us

live next
has all we

B♭

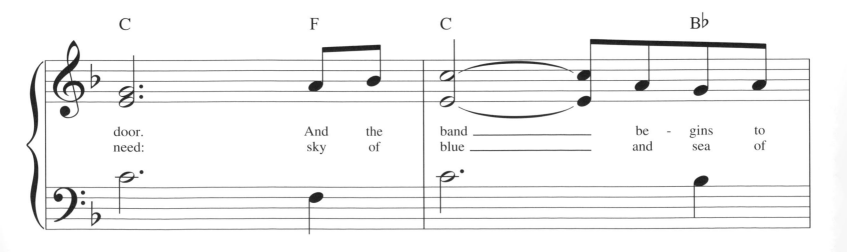

C door.
need:

And the
sky of

F

C band _____ be - gins to
blue _____ and sea of

B♭

YESTERDAY

Words and Music by JOHN LENNON
and PAUL McCARTNEY

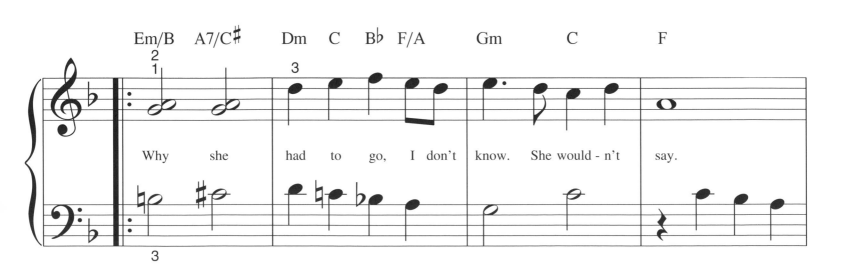

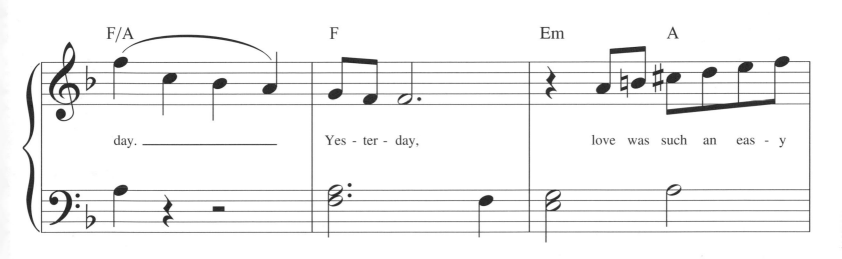

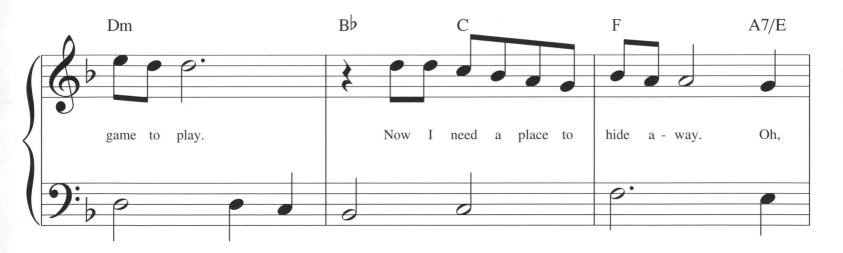

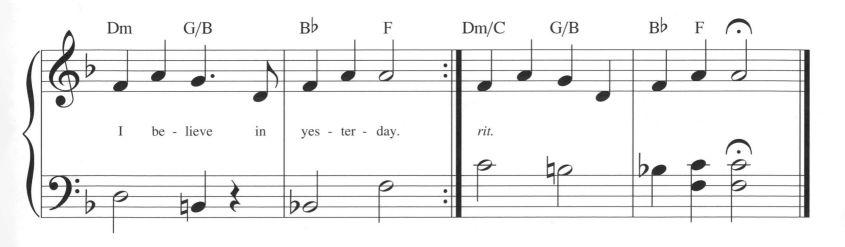

YOU WON'T SEE ME

Words and Music by JOHN LENNON
and PAUL McCARTNEY

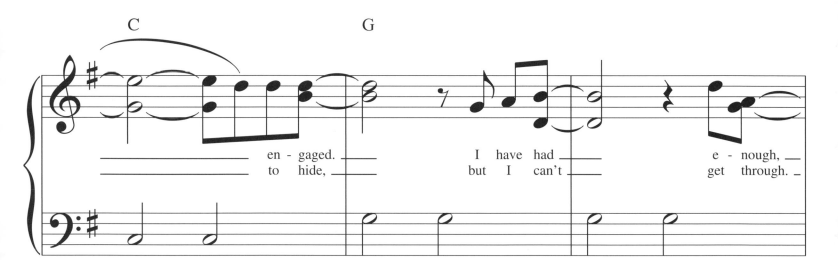

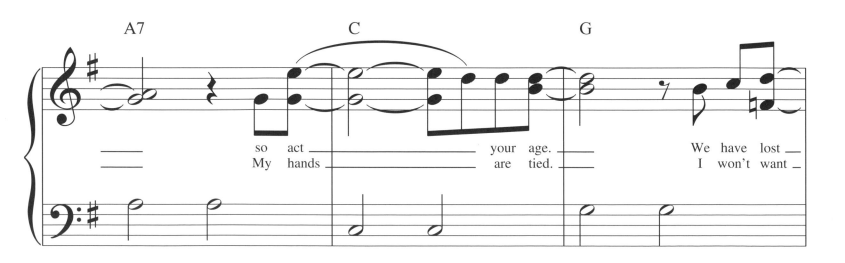

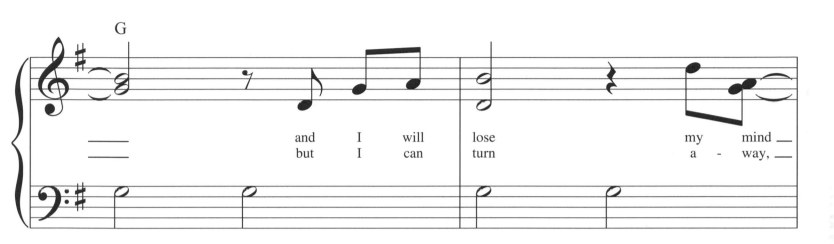

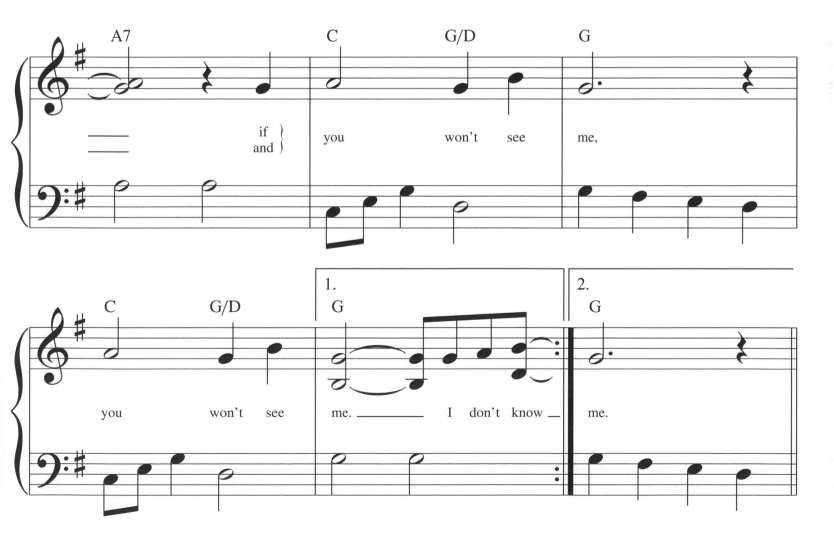

Time af - ter time ___ you re - fuse ___ to e - ven lis -

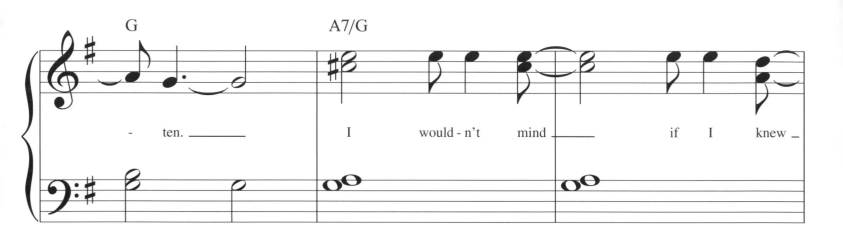

- ten. ___ I would - n't mind ___ if I knew ___

___ what I ___ was miss - ing. Though the days ___ are few, ___

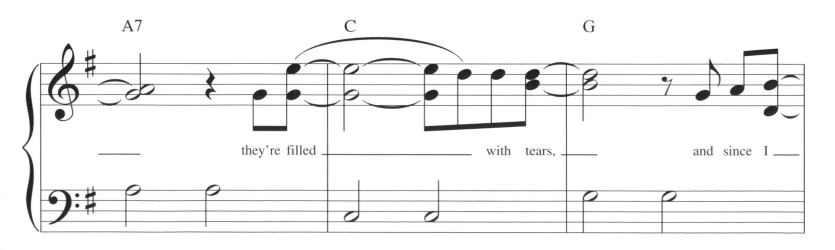

___ they're filled ___ with tears, ___ and since I ___

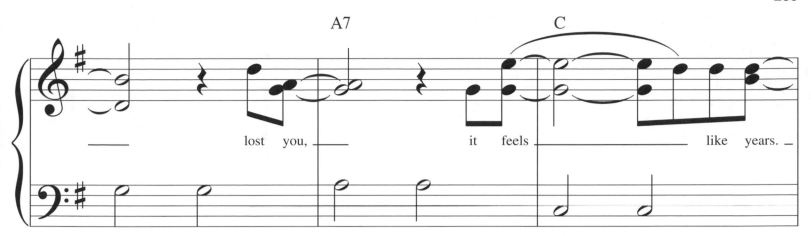

lost you, _____ it feels _____ like years. ___

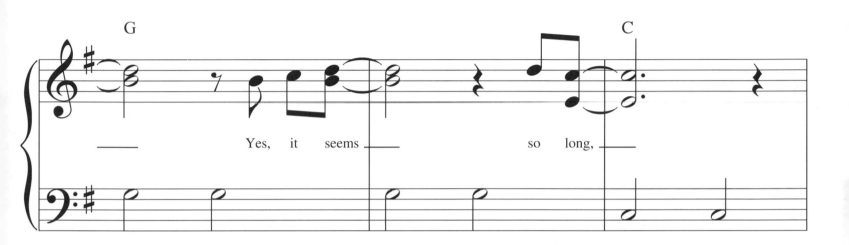

Yes, it seems _____ so long, ___

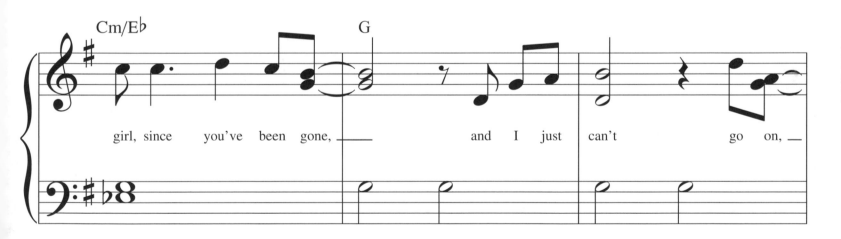

girl, since you've been gone, ___ and I just can't go on, ___

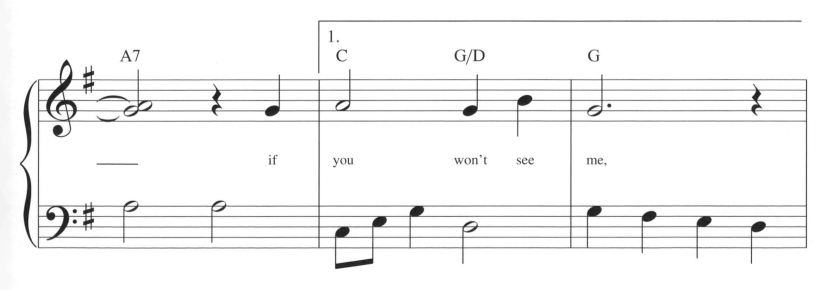

if you won't see me,

YOU'VE GOT TO HIDE YOUR LOVE AWAY

Words and Music by JOHN LENNON
and PAUL McCARTNEY

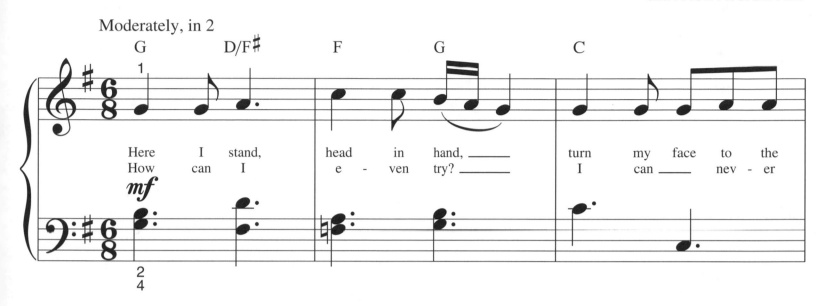

Here I stand, head in hand, ____ turn my face to the
How can I e - ven try? ____ I can ____ nev - er

wall. If she's gone, I can't go on ____
win. Hear - ing them, see - ing them, ____

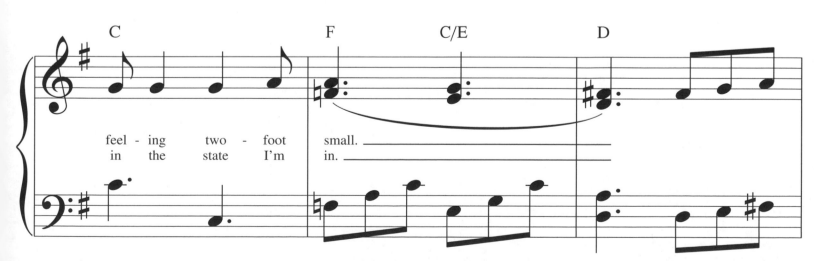

feel - ing two - foot small. ____
in the state I'm in. ____